Deforestation Exposed: Trees, Truths, and Tomorrow

Written by:
Alan E Shields

INDEX

Introduction

The Role of Forests

Forests, often referred to as the lungs of our planet, serve an indispensable role in sustaining life on Earth. But to understand them merely as oxygen producers is to miss the vast tapestry of interactions and benefits they offer.

The process of photosynthesis, where forests absorb carbon dioxide and release life-sustaining oxygen, is just the beginning of the story. The vast expanses of green cloak our planet in areas we might never see but whose influence we feel daily. Forests are much more than a congregation of trees; they are complex, dynamic, and vibrant systems humming with life, each tree communicating, cooperating, and competing in a bustling world of its own.

- **Biodiversity Reservoirs**: Venture into a forest, and you step into a world bursting with life. Forests are home to over 80% of terrestrial species. This dazzling array includes mammals that roam the forest floors, birds that echo their calls from the canopy, insects that pollinate, plants that offer a smorgasbord of medicinal properties, and fungi that decompose and recycle nutrients. Each of these organisms, from the towering elephant to the inconspicuous beetle, plays a pivotal role in maintaining the equilibrium of the ecosystem. Their interconnected relationships form a web of life so intricate that the removal of one strand can unravel countless others.

- **Climate Regulation**: Forests are Earth's thermostat. Their vast canopies absorb sunlight, providing shade and cooling the land beneath. Through a process called transpiration, they release water vapor, which plays a crucial role in atmospheric cooling and cloud formation. This not only influences local climates but has ramifications on global weather patterns. The roots of trees, intertwined and sprawling, anchor soil, preventing erosion and mitigating the devastating impacts of floods by acting as natural buffers, soaking up excess water and releasing it slowly.

- **Human Livelihoods**: The silent whispers of the forests tell tales of human civilizations that have thrived in their embrace. Over 1.6 billion people, a significant portion of humanity, depend on forests for their very survival. This encompasses the indigenous and tribal communities whose lives are intricately woven with forests, respecting its rhythms and reaping its bounty sustainably. Beyond these immediate dwellers, forests fuel global industries. The timber that builds homes, the paper on which history is written, and the medicinal compounds that heal are all gifts from the forest.

- **Cultural Significance**: Forests are the settings of legends, the sanctuaries of deities, and the playgrounds of spirits. They have held a mirror to human emotions and aspirations, shaping our artistic and spiritual endeavors. In the sacred groves of India, every rustling leaf and murmuring brook is believed to be infused with the divine. The dense woods of European folklore, with their enchanting and sometimes menacing allure, have been the backdrop for tales that have enthralled generations.

From rituals to celebrations, from reverence to fear, forests have been at the epicenter, shaping human consciousness, reminding us of the eternal bond between man and nature.

Scope of the Book

As we turn the pages of this book, we find ourselves at the doorstep of a vast, often shadowed world that is the narrative of deforestation. The layers of this narrative are as intricate and intertwined as the roots of an ancient tree, and unraveling them demands a deep dive into the annals of time, society, and human ambition.

From the first stroke of an axe against a primordial tree to the roar of chainsaws in today's dwindling forests, deforestation has been an ominous constant. The ensuing chapters don't merely chronicle events but aim to weave the intricate tapestry of causes, players, and repercussions. Every cleared patch of forest is not just a loss of green but a disturbance in the intricate web of life, sending ripples across ecosystems, economies, and societies.

Central to our exploration is the machinery of human desire and its consequences. We'll dissect the anatomy of corporate ambitions, where balance sheets often weigh heavier than ecological balance. Here, the tall, unyielding trees are seen not as sentinels of nature, but as commodities to be harvested, often with little foresight into the cascading effects of such actions.

But it's not just the corporations. Our own roles, as consumers, as voters, as silent witnesses, come under scrutiny. How have our demands, sometimes born out of ignorance and at other times, indifference, contributed to the narrative? And in the hallways of power, we'll shine a light on policies, or the lack thereof, that have been both a shield and a sword in the battle against deforestation.

Yet, amid the tales of loss and greed, there are stories that kindle hope. Narratives of communities that have stood as bulwarks against the onslaught, of innovators who are carving out paths of coexistence, and of places where the forests are rising again.

This book is not just an account; it's an invitation — to understand, to care, and to act. It's a clarion call to recognize the urgency, to be informed about the stakes, and to be part of the chorus that demands a halt to the devastation and envisions a greener, more harmonious world.

Historical Perspective

As old as time itself, the tale of forests and humanity is one of kinship, survival, and ultimately, dominion. The towering trees, with their branches reaching out to the skies and roots delving deep into the Earth, have borne silent witness to the evolution of humankind, from our primitive days to our current epoch of technological marvels.

Imagine, if you will, the dawn of humanity. Early humans, with their nascent understanding of the world, found in forests a haven—a sanctuary that protected them from the elements, predators, and the unknown. The dense canopies, with their mosaic of light and shade, cradled these early societies, offering them not just shelter, but a veritable treasure trove. Berries, nuts, game, and medicinal herbs—all life essentials were at their fingertips. Every rustle, every bird call, every changing season imparted wisdom about nature's rhythms and secrets.

But as the wheel of time turned, so did the dynamics of this bond. With the dawn of agriculture, humanity's first major innovation, the forests faced their initial challenge. The fertile lands they cloistered became the very target of early societies eager to sow, cultivate, and harvest. As communities blossomed into civilizations, the scales of dependency shifted. Monumental entities like the Maya in the heart of Mesoamerica or the enigmatic Khmer Empire of Southeast Asia began to stretch their arms further into forested domains. And in their wake, they left not just architectural marvels but also scars of overexploitation, which historians and ecologists now believe contributed to their mysterious declines.

The relentless march of time brought new challenges for our verdant guardians. The age of discovery and the rise of empires cast avaricious eyes on lucrative forest resources. The scent of cedar from the expansive forests of the Middle East wafted across ancient trade routes, heralding their use in ambitious projects like shipbuilding. As if echoing through time, the same appetite for exploitation manifests today in the depths of the Amazon. Only now, the tools of extraction are far more potent, and the demand, fueled by a globalized world's insatiable appetite, is ceaseless.

In many ways, the story of forests is the story of humanity's evolution—from reverence to dominion, from coexistence to exploitation. It's a tale told in the rings of ancient trees, in the annals of lost civilizations, and in the modern-day challenges of conservation. As we navigate the chapters that lie ahead, we'll traverse this intricate timeline, shedding light on the multifaceted relationship between humanity and forests, highlighting the reverence they once commanded and the reckoning they now face in our hands.

Historical Context

Ancient Practices

In the vast tapestry of human history, forests have always occupied a significant place, their silent shadows holding the stories of countless generations. Since the earliest days, these lush landscapes have provided a backdrop to humanity's evolving narrative, bearing witness to our triumphs, our innovations, and at times, our insensitivities.

With the first steps of human civilization, when our ancestors progressed from nomadic wanderings to establishing roots, forests became the cornerstone of burgeoning societies. Initially, the symbiotic relationship between humans and forests was apparent: forests provided resources, and humans, in their primal ways, would sometimes give back by means of rituals, or merely by not taking more than needed. But as necessity beckoned and our understanding of the land grew, the scales of this relationship began to tip.

- **Slash and Burn Agriculture**: Among the earliest forms of structured agriculture was the slash and burn technique. Imagine the scene: communities banding together, the sharp sounds of axes felling trees, and then, the sight of fires consuming the dry timber, releasing plumes of smoke into the sky. These flames, while destructive, bore promise. The ashes left behind, a powdery grey testament to the trees that once stood, enriched the soil beneath. Crops would be planted, and for a few seasons, the land would yield bountiful harvests. But the very essence of this method was transience. Soil, despite the initial boost from the ashes, would wane in fertility over time. And with that, communities would migrate, seeking new patches of forest to begin the cycle anew. In the epochs of low population densities, when vast swathes of untouched forests still blanketed the earth, this method had its own rhythm and balance. But with the ticking clock of time and the swell of human numbers, the intervals between these shifts shortened. What was once a dance with nature began to resemble a race, with sustainability slipping through the gaps.

- **Early Civilizations and Deforestation**: As we cast our gaze further down the corridors of time, we encounter the grandeur of ancient civilizations, each a testament to human ingenuity and ambition. The mighty Mayans, with their sprawling cities and intricate calendars, or the Greeks, with their pantheon of gods and birth of democracy, carved their stories not just in stone and parchment but also in the very landscape. Forests, in their quest for expansion, were often the collateral. Trees made way for grand edifices, firewood, ships, and farmlands. This rapid pace of deforestation, historians and ecologists now postulate, might not have been without consequences. The very ecosystems these civilizations thrived upon began to falter. Water sources dwindled, soils eroded, and crop yields became unpredictable. In these ecological upheavals, we find clues pointing towards the decline, and in some cases, the dramatic collapse of civilizations that once stood as unyielding testaments to human prowess. The forests, in their silent wisdom, had perhaps given an early lesson on the delicate balance of existence—a lesson that resonates even today as we grapple with the challenges of deforestation.

Industrial Revolution

A smog-filled sky, the cacophony of machinery, and the burgeoning rise of urban landscapes characterize one of the most transformative periods in human history: The Industrial Revolution. While it is celebrated as an era of unprecedented technological advancements and economic progress, it also heralded an intensified assault on the world's forests, turning them from revered sanctuaries into mere commodities.

This epoch, spanning the 18th to the 19th centuries, wasn't just about steam engines, cotton gins, or the telegraph. At its heart, it represented a shift in ethos—a departure from traditional, more sustainable ways of living to a relentless pursuit of industrial progress. And forests, with their vast resources, became the collateral damage in this headlong rush.

- **Fuel for the Fire**: Picture this—a factory in the heart of England with tall chimneys belching out smoke. Inside, the roar of steam-powered engines dominates, driving the machinery that would weave, mint, or forge. These machines had a voracious appetite, an unquenchable thirst, and it was wood that stoked these flames. Forests, especially in the early days of the revolution before the broad adoption of coal, were seen less as intricate ecosystems and more as vast stockpiles of fuel. As industries proliferated, they gnawed away at woodland edges, converting verdant expanses into barren lands, all to ensure that the heart of the industrial machine kept beating.

- **Timber Demand**: But the appetite of the revolution wasn't restricted to fuel alone. As urban centers burgeoned, becoming the nerve centers of commerce and innovation, the skylines began to change. Brick, mortar, and especially wood became the materials of choice. Every new building, be it a residence or a factory, and every expanding railroad demanded timber. And it wasn't just the quantity that was staggering. The practices of the loggers, dictated more by urgency than prudence, were marked by profligacy. Forests were felled indiscriminately, and only the "perfect" logs made the cut, while vast quantities were discarded, deemed unsuitable. This wastefulness, coupled with an ever-increasing demand, led to forests receding at an unprecedented rate.

- **Colonial Exploits**: While the heart of the Industrial Revolution pulsed in Europe, its ramifications echoed across oceans and continents, particularly in regions under the yoke of colonial powers. Colonial ambitions, ever eager to fuel the industries back home, cast avaricious eyes upon the verdant riches of Asia, Africa, and the Americas. Trees were felled, not for the benefit of local populations, but to satiate the hunger of European industries. Majestic teak from Burma, mahogany from the Caribbean, and countless other species were shipped to European shores. But the colonial assault wasn't just about extraction. As forests were cleared, the lands were repurposed for another venture: plantations. Vast stretches, once shadowed by canopies, now basked in sunlight, bearing monocultures of tea, rubber, or coffee—all cash crops meant for export. The local ecology and the indigenous communities, who had for centuries lived in harmony with these forests, faced displacement and disruption, becoming footnotes in the grand narrative of industrial progress.

The Industrial Revolution, for all its technological marvels and societal transformations, also carries with it a legacy of exploitation. As smokestacks reached for the skies and railroads crisscrossed continents, they left in their wake a world grappling with the consequences of unrestrained progress. The forests, with their silent resilience, serve as both a reminder of what was lost and a beacon of hope for a more balanced future.

Globalization and its Effects

As the world ushered in the 20th century, it stood on the cusp of yet another monumental transformation. The steady thrum of machinery from the Industrial Revolution was giving way to the harmonious symphony of globalization. The world was shrinking, not in its vast expanse, but in its interconnectedness. Oceans were no longer barriers but bridges, linking economies, cultures, and ideologies. This era was marked by burgeoning cities, technological marvels, and a dream of a united world. But with these dreams came shadows that often darkened the very lands that bore the brunt of global consumerism: our forests.

- **Rise in Consumer Demand**: Picture a family in the suburbs of America or a bustling apartment in Europe during the mid-20th century. The drawing rooms adorned with wooden furniture, daily groceries containing products like palm oil, or the increasing demand for paper and packaging. This rise in consumerism was not isolated to any one region; it was a global phenomenon. As populations surged and living standards improved, there was an insatiable appetite for goods. This appetite often had its roots in far-off lands. The teak for the dining table might have originated in the forests of

Southeast Asia, the beef in the freezer from the cleared lands of the Amazon. This global demand for products was a significant driver behind large-scale deforestation, especially in ecologically sensitive areas. Regions like the Amazon in South America or the rainforests in Borneo were stripped to cater to a consumer thousands of miles away, often unaware of the ecological price of their purchase.

- **Transnational Corporations**: As capital took wings, corporations, no longer tethered to their countries of origin, began to spread their operations across the globe. In this new world order, where profit margins often dictated policies, many companies sought lands where production costs were low, and regulatory oversight was lax. Forests, especially in countries with weaker environmental regulations, became prime targets. Expansive stretches of green were converted to plantations, mines, or factories. The notion of sustainable harvesting or environmental responsibility often took a backseat, with balance sheets and stock prices guiding actions. The unchecked power and reach of these corporations meant that by the time the local environmental impact became apparent, the damage was often irreversible.

- **Land Rights and Indigenous Communities**: Nestled deep within these forests were communities that had called these lands home for centuries. Their lives, cultures, and beliefs were interwoven with the trees, rivers, and animals around them. But as the wheels of globalization churned, these indigenous communities found themselves at the crossroads of progress and preservation. Lands that had been preserved through sustainable practices were eyed by corporations and governments alike. Ancestral domains were demarcated, often without consent, for logging or plantations. The very trees that were considered sacred were felled, and rivers that had nurtured them were polluted. The displacement of these communities and the erasure of their practices added a cultural and human tragedy to the environmental catastrophe.

In its essence, globalization, with its promise of a connected world, also magnified the age-old conundrum: progress at what cost? As trade barriers fell and markets opened, the very ecosystems that sustain life were imperiled. The tale of deforestation in the era of globalization serves as a poignant reminder of the delicate balance between growth, responsibility, and sustainability.

Mythology and Religion

From the dense rainforests echoing with whispers of ancient tribes to the solitary oaks standing tall in vast plains, forests and trees have been etched into the very soul of human spirituality and mythology. Their leaves have rustled with stories, their trunks have borne the scars of countless rites, and in their shade, seekers have found wisdom. A dive into the archives of human history reveals just how intrinsic this connection between man, myth, and forest truly is.

- **The Norse Yggdrasil**: In the icy landscapes of the North, where nights could last months and auroras painted the sky, the Norse civilizations envisioned the cosmos as a colossal, evergreen tree named Yggdrasil. Unlike any ordinary tree, Yggdrasil's sprawling branches and deep roots weren't confined to Midgard, the realm of humans. They stretched into the heavens, where gods resided, and plunged into the subterranean worlds of the dead. Each realm, from the abode of the Aesir gods to the chilling Hel, found its place in this cosmic tree. Yggdrasil was more than just wood and leaf; it was the embodiment of the interconnectedness of life, death, fate, and rebirth. It reminds us that forests, in their silent wisdom, often mirror the very design of existence, connecting realms and realities.

- **The Bodhi Tree in Buddhism**: Far from the fjords of Scandinavia, in the heart of ancient India, a prince named Siddhartha sat under the shade of a Bodhi tree, seeking answers to the suffering he witnessed. The tree, with its heart-shaped leaves, bore witness to a spiritual journey that would reshape the world. After days of deep meditation, beneath its sprawling canopy, Siddhartha attained enlightenment, becoming the Buddha. Today, the Bodhi tree stands as a symbol of spiritual awakening in Buddhism. Pilgrims from across the globe visit Bodh Gaya, where the original tree stood, seeking blessings and insights. The reverence for the Bodhi tree underscores the idea that forests and trees can be portals to higher truths and spiritual realizations.

- **Celtic Sacred Groves**: The verdant landscapes of Europe, with their dense woodlands and mystic meadows, were home to the Celts. For them, nature wasn't just a provider but a realm brimming with spirits and deities. Groves, clusters of trees often surrounding clearings, were considered especially sacred. It was believed that these groves were liminal spaces, thin boundaries between the mortal world and the realm of the divine. Druids, the priestly class among Celts, performed their rituals in these groves, seeking blessings, divining the future, or propitiating deities. The sacred groves highlight the belief that forests can be conduits, places where the divine touches the earth, and where prayers ascend to the heavens.

The stories from Norse lands, Buddhist traditions, and Celtic woods are but a few threads in the rich tapestry of human history interwoven with forests. They serve as reminders that beyond their ecological significance, forests have cradled our spiritual and mythological narratives, shaping civilizations, beliefs, and the very essence of our being.

While these stories and beliefs illustrate a profound respect for trees and forests, the irony lies in our actions, which often run counter to these revered tales. As we delve deeper into the subsequent chapters, this dichotomy between reverence in belief and ruthlessness in action becomes all too evident

Cultural and Historical Ties to Forests

Mythology and Religion

From the dawn of storytelling, forests have been a cornerstone of our collective imagination. Their expansive canopies, mysterious depths, and ever-present whispers of leaves have birthed stories that traverse the spectrum from reverence to fear, from birth to death, and from the mundane to the divine.

- **Sacred Groves**: Throughout history, particular sections of forests were cordoned off from the routine of human activity, declared sacred, and were revered as pockets of the divine on Earth. These were the sacred groves. In ancient Celtic traditions, for instance, these groves were far more than just clusters of trees; they were bustling with the presence of spirits and gods. Druids, the Celtic priests, would hold their mystical ceremonies within these hallowed groves, often during specific phases of the moon or during solstices, believing that these woods amplified their connection to the cosmos. A similar reverence can be found in India, where even today, in the midst of rapid urbanization, small patches of forests or even singular trees are often cordoned off with colorful threads, denoting their sanctity and protecting them from harm.

- **Symbolism of Trees**: Throughout human history, trees have been more than just passive entities dotting our landscapes; they've been powerful symbols, each telling a tale of its own. The Norse revered Yggdrasil, a colossal tree that connected various realms, its roots and branches holding the cosmos together. It stood as a symbol of life's interconnectedness and the cycles of birth, death, and rebirth. In contrast, Christianity's Tree of Knowledge in the Garden of Eden became a symbol of temptation, knowledge, and the fall of man. The Bodhi tree, with its heart-shaped leaves, not only marked the place where Siddhartha Gautama attained enlightenment but became a symbol for Buddhists worldwide of the potential for inner transformation and enlightenment that lies within us all.

- **Forests in Folktales**: The hallowed pages of folktales and fairy tales across cultures are dappled with the shadows of dense forests. These woods are places where the ordinary meets the extraordinary. In the haunting tales of the Brothers Grimm, the Black Forest of Germany comes alive with witches, fairies, and wolves, serving as a backdrop where human virtues and vices are put to the test. Similarly, the dense, snow-covered woods in Russian folktales become realms where Baba Yaga, the witch, might lure you into her hut on chicken legs.

- **Mysticism and Forests**: Time and again, when the material world became too chaotic or distracting, spiritual seekers would find solace in the embrace of the woods. Forests, with their serene ambiance and distance from human settlements, were seen as spaces of profound spiritual energy. In various religious traditions, from the Christian hermits and saints who meditated in the solitude of the wilderness to the Hindu sages or 'rishis' of India who retreated to forest ashrams for deep meditation, forests were the chosen abodes. They were places of quiet, introspection, and profound revelations, where the veil between the mortal and the divine seemed thin and permeable.

In every whispered wind through the trees and every path that meanders through the woods, there's a story, a belief, or a legend waiting to be told. Forests, in all their grandeur, have been our companions in the journey of understanding the world, the divine, and ourselves.

Historical Dependence

From the first human civilizations to the complex societies of today, forests have played a pivotal role, intertwining deeply with the fabric of human existence and civilization's development.

- **Shelter and Building**: The proximity of ancient human settlements to forests wasn't just a matter of chance; it was a strategic decision for survival. The dense thickets offered protection against predators and harsh weather, while also providing abundant resources for building. Early humans used rudimentary tools to shape logs and branches into shelters, laying the foundations for architecture as we know it today. As civilizations evolved, so did their architectural prowess. The ancient city of Mohenjo-Daro, a jewel of the Indus Valley Civilization, stands testament to this. Excavations reveal wooden beams used to fortify brick structures and intricate wooden drainage systems, underscoring the integral role of forests in ancient city planning and infrastructure. Moreover, not just structures, forests provided raw materials for tools, vehicles, and even art.

- **Food and Medicine**: Beyond their role as protectors or providers of shelter, forests have been pantries and pharmacies for millennia. Dense undergrowth teems with fruits, nuts, and edible plants that became staples in early human diets. The lush green canopy concealed not only sources of nutrition but also game, making forests prime hunting grounds. And when disease or injury struck, it was to the forest that our ancestors turned. The indigenous tribes of the Amazon, with their vast ethnobotanical knowledge, recognized the healing potential of thousands of plant species, some venomous to the touch, yet curative when prepared rightly. This ancient wisdom, transmitted orally across generations, has shaped the landscape of modern pharmacology, giving us drugs like quinine for malaria from the bark of the cinchona tree.

- **Cultural Significance**: As human societies grew more complex, so did their relationship with forests, which began to hold profound cultural and spiritual importance. In the dense woods of ancient Europe, the Druids, with their white robes and golden sickles, would gather in clearings under the moonlight, conducting ceremonies and seeking prophecies. Across the ocean, the Native American tribes revered the spirits of the forest, performing intricate dances and songs that echoed the rustling of leaves and the calls of the forest animals. These rituals, ceremonies, and beliefs rooted in forests not only connected these societies to nature but also helped instill values, norms, and societal structures.

- **Trade and Economy**: The emerald expanses of forests weren't just havens of biodiversity; they were goldmines for early economies. The aromatic resins from the trees of the Arabian Peninsula, the myriad spices from the dense woods of the Malabar coast in India, and the precious medicinal herbs from the heart of China were all sought-after commodities. These forest products became central to intricate trade networks, fostering economic and cultural exchanges. The Silk Road, though famously named after the delicate threads, was more than just a route for silk. Caravans laden with forest-derived products like sandalwood, frankincense, and myrrh traversed these routes, connecting distant civilizations, fostering diplomatic ties, and even facilitating the spread of ideas and religions.

Through each of these facets of historical dependence, it becomes evident that forests have not just been passive backdrops but active participants in the narrative of human history.

However, this dependence was not always benign. As civilizations grew and expanded, their needs often led to overexploitation. The once-thriving civilizations of Easter Island and the Mayans, for instance, faced decline due to unsustainable practices which led to deforestation, showcasing the fragile balance between human progress and environmental sustainability.

The Underlying Causes

Economic Drivers

The intricate web of global economics, with its pulsing veins of supply chains, market demands, and relentless pursuits of profits, intersects powerfully with the health and well-being of our world's forests. At this crossroad, we find that economic imperatives, more often than not, lead to decisions that favor immediate gains over long-term ecological stability.

- **Timber Industry**: Timber, with its versatility and durability, has been an invaluable resource for humanity. The skyscrapers of modern cities, the cozy suburban homes, the books that chronicle our history, and the furniture that adds comfort to our lives all trace their origins back to forests. The global timber industry, a multi-billion dollar sector, relies heavily on vast tracts of forests. And while the narrative often revolves around the need for timber, the reality of extraction paints a more troubling picture. Beyond just the removal of trees, the infrastructure to support logging, such as roads, further fragments the forests and disrupts animal habitats. Furthermore, many regions with high logging activities often witness a spiral of other destructive practices. Once roads are built, they provide access to poachers, further mining activities, and more, exponentially magnifying the environmental footprint.

- **Agricultural Expansion**: With the clockwork regularity of harvest seasons, agriculture has been the backbone of human civilizations. But the scale and intensity of modern agriculture, driven by the need to feed an ever-growing global population, have translated into a war against forests. Clearing forests for agriculture isn't a mere act of cutting down trees; it represents a shift from a diverse, multi-layered ecosystem to often simplified, single-crop fields. This simplification comes at the cost of soil health, water quality, and local climate regulation. Monocultures, with their vast stretches of identical crops, not only diminish biodiversity but also make the entire system vulnerable to pests and diseases, leading to an increased reliance on chemical pesticides and fertilizers.

- **Soy, Beef, and Palm Oil**: The interplay between consumer demand and forest health becomes even more pronounced when we delve into specific industries. Take the Amazon rainforest, a treasure trove of biodiversity, often termed 'the lungs of the Earth'. Here, the demand for soy and beef has driven deforestation at rates that were once unimaginable. Vast stretches of ancient trees are felled, the land cleared and torched, only to be replaced by soy plantations. But this soy doesn't always end up on human plates. A significant chunk is channeled into feeding livestock, primarily cattle. The beef industry, especially in regions like Brazil, is a major driver of deforestation. The equation is simple yet tragic: more global demand for beef equals more pastures, leading to more trees being cut. Meanwhile, in the archipelagos of Southeast Asia, another crisis unfolds. Native forests, some of the most biodiverse regions on Earth, are being rapidly replaced by monotonous stretches of palm oil plantations. The ubiquitous nature of palm oil in modern products, from chocolates to cosmetics, fuels this destructive conversion.

In the heart of these economic drivers, a fundamental question emerges: Can the principles of supply and demand coexist with ecological sustainability? The challenge lies in reconciling our economic aspirations with the imperatives of a planet that has finite resources.

Political Dynamics

The intertwined narratives of politics and forests offer a revealing glimpse into how power structures, governance models, and political agendas can profoundly impact the environment. At the heart of political decisions lies a complex interplay of interests, be they economic, ideological, or simply rooted in the quest for continued power. When such interests do not align with environmental sustainability, the consequences for forests can be dire.

- **Short-sighted Policies**: The realm of politics often operates in cycles dictated by election terms, which can result in a myopic view of development. Governments, especially those facing economic pressures or seeking to showcase rapid progress, might opt for policies that promise immediate returns. Granting licenses for mining projects, large-scale agriculture, or logging in forested areas might boost GDP figures or employment rates in the short term, making for impressive political report cards. However, these short-term gains frequently overshadow the long-term ecological costs, such as loss of biodiversity, soil erosion, and disrupted water cycles. Absent or rushed environmental impact assessments further compound the problem, allowing projects to proceed without fully understanding their ramifications.

- **Corruption**: The tendrils of corruption can choke even the most well-intentioned regulations. In countries where corruption is endemic, illegal logging often becomes a lucrative, low-risk venture for both perpetrators and complicit officials. But this isn't just about a few bribes exchanged in shadowy corners. It represents a deep erosion of trust and governance. For local communities who rely on forests, this corruption can mean the loss of their homes, livelihoods, and a sense of security. Moreover, it discourages international collaboration and trust, especially when global efforts are being made to conserve forests and combat climate change.

- **Weak Governance**: Beyond overt corruption, the mere absence of robust governance structures can leave forests vulnerable. This isn't merely about having laws on paper, but the capability and will to enforce them. In regions where governance is fragile, monitoring vast forested areas becomes a Herculean task, often marred by inadequate resources, lack of trained personnel, and in some cases, threats from powerful illegal logging mafias. These forests, left at the mercy of unchecked human activities, suffer not just from logging but also other illegal activities, including wildlife poaching and unauthorized land encroachments. The cascading effects of such activities disrupt local ecosystems, endanger species, and further marginalize already vulnerable indigenous communities.

When political dynamics fail to prioritize or protect forests, it's not just the trees that suffer. The repercussions ripple out, affecting local communities, regional ecologies, and the global fight against climate change. Thus, integrating forest conservation into the core of political agendas isn't merely an environmental necessity; it's a testament to good governance, foresight, and responsible leadership.

Social Factors

The deep-seated relationship between society and forests is a tale as old as civilization itself. As societies evolve, so do their interactions with the environment, revealing a mosaic of influences, beliefs, and imperatives that shape the destiny of our green expanses.

- **Population Growth**: The exponential growth in global population has catalyzed a cascading demand for resources. Every individual requires shelter, food, clothing, and other essentials, the procurement of which directly or indirectly impinges upon forest resources. The simple mathematics of catering to nearly 8 billion humans (and counting) exerts colossal pressure on our ecosystems. When one thinks of burgeoning populations, it's not just the immediate demand for land or timber; it's the infrastructural development, increased food production, expanded transportation networks, and much more. Each aspect, while crucial for human welfare, poses questions about sustainability and the delicate balance between development and conservation.

- **Urbanization**: The allure of urban life, often painted with broad strokes of prosperity, opportunities, and modernity, has seen a mass migration from rural to urban areas over the past few decades. Cities, historically seen as hubs of innovation, culture, and economic activity, have swelled beyond their boundaries. This rapid urban expansion, however, comes at a cost. Forests on the city fringes are cleared to make way for housing projects, commercial centers, and transportation corridors. Beyond just the loss of trees, this also disrupts wildlife habitats, leading to phenomena like human-animal conflicts. Furthermore, the infrastructure to support growing urban populations, such as water reservoirs or highways, often necessitates further intrusions into forested lands.

- **Cultural Perspectives**: Societal values, often interwoven with historical, spiritual, and cultural narratives, play a profound role in shaping attitudes towards forests. In certain cultures or communities, clearing a patch of forest to make land arable or building a home might be a rite of passage, symbolizing an individual's progression in life. In others, showcasing wooden artifacts or constructing grand edifices from rare woods might be a status symbol, reflecting affluence and power. While these practices might be deeply entrenched, they sometimes perpetuate a paradigm where nature is seen as a resource to be dominated or exploited, rather than a cohabitant to be respected. It's crucial to understand that these aren't merely 'backward' or 'traditional' practices. Even in modern societies, the rush for exotic wooden furniture or sprawling sea-facing homes carved out of coastal forests reflects a similar ethos.

The essence of addressing the social factors driving deforestation lies in recognizing these nuances and initiating conversations. It's about building bridges of understanding and fostering a collective consciousness that values forests for what they truly are: lifelines.

International Pressures

We live in an era defined by globalization, a time when the tremors of decisions made in one corner of the world can be felt in another. Forest ecosystems, in all their rich biodiversity and ecological complexity, aren't immune to these global influences. The dynamics of international trade, market demands, and investments intertwine to weave a narrative that, for all its economic prospects, raises profound questions about sustainability and environmental ethics.

- **Trade Dynamics**: International trade stands at the crossroads where economics, politics, and ecology meet. Free trade agreements and global commerce networks have facilitated the exchange of goods at an unprecedented scale. However, this seamless exchange comes with environmental strings attached. Timber, agricultural products, and myriad other goods produced by encroaching upon or exploiting forests find their way into international markets. Despite various certifications and labels aiming to assure ethical sourcing, the reality can sometimes be an intricate web of supply chains, where the ecological cost is obscured. Nations, in the quest for economic advancement, sometimes make concessions in environmental regulations to remain competitive in global markets, a dynamic that underscores the urgent need for embedding sustainability in international trade norms.

- **Global Market Demands**: In a world shaped by consumerism, the adage 'consumer is king' resonates deeply. However, it also brings into focus the responsibility that lies with the crown. The sprawling supermarkets stocked with exotic woods, paper products, and an array of foods are a testament to global market demands. But behind every product is a story – a narrative of extraction, production, and transportation, each phase imprinting on our planet. Countries, especially those rich in forest resources, are caught in a delicate balance of catering to global demands while safeguarding their ecological treasures. It is a dance of economics and ecology, and often, the music is tuned to the melodies of market demands.

- **International Investments**: The infusion of foreign capital can be a lifeline for developing economies. Multinational corporations, with their financial prowess, can foster growth, employment, and development. However, there lies a paradox. Many of these investments, especially in sectors like mining, agriculture, and infrastructure, are funneled into projects that necessitate extensive deforestation. Countries with burgeoning populations and development aspirations can find themselves in a quandary, navigating the tightrope between economic growth and ecological preservation. In nations where environmental regulations are lenient or enforcement is lax, the equation becomes all the more complex. Forests, in their silent majesty, often bear the brunt of this complex interplay of international economics and politics.

In encapsulating the issue of international pressures and deforestation, we embark upon a journey that isn't just rooted in ecology but extends into the realms of economics, politics, ethics, and beyond. Every piece of timber, every product sourced from these serene yet vulnerable ecosystems, echoes the intricate dance of global forces, narrating a tale that is as profound as it is urgent. In this narrative, every consumer, policy-maker, and investor plays a part, and the script is written with every choice made, every policy enacted, and every dollar invested.

34

The Environmental Impact

Biodiversity Loss

Forests, in all their lush expanse and rich tapestry of life, are more than just clusters of trees. They are dynamic realms where every leaf, insect, bird, and mammal tells a story of coexistence and evolution. Their resilience and diversity are astounding. Yet, as swathes of forests vanish, the intricate symphony of life within them faces a deafening silence, leading to an irreplaceable loss of biodiversity.

- **Threatened Species**: The magnitude of the threat that deforestation poses to species is profound. From the towering trees that form the forest canopy to the smallest insects that inhabit its floor, each species is a chapter in an ancient story of evolution. The orangutans of Borneo, with their intelligent eyes and human-like expressions, have over the years become the poignant symbols of the cost of deforestation. Their habitats are shrinking, pushing them closer to the brink of extinction. Similarly, the enigmatic jaguars of the Amazon, the apex predators of their realm, now roam in ever-shrinking territories, often coming into conflict with human settlements. And these are just the species we know of. Countless others, still hidden in the depths of these forests, unknown to science, face a silent end even before they're discovered.

- **Ripple Effect**: Ecosystems operate in delicate balance, maintained through complex interrelationships between its inhabitants. Remove one link, and the entire chain can unravel.

Take, for instance, a specific bird species that feeds on certain pests. The loss of this bird due to deforestation can lead to an explosion in the pest population, which in turn can decimate the plants they feed on. This domino effect can alter the very character of an ecosystem, leading to imbalances that are often irreversible. The nuanced dance of predator and prey, of pollinator and flower, of soil bacterium and root, when disrupted, sings a dirge of ecological disarray.

- **Genetic Diversity**: Beyond the evident loss of species, there's a less visible, yet equally significant loss — that of genetic diversity. Every individual of a species carries a unique set of genes, shaped by millennia of evolution. These genes are the blueprints of life, determining how an organism grows, how it responds to challenges, and how it reproduces. As forests diminish, populations of species dwindle, leading to a genetic bottleneck. This reduced genetic variability means that the species has fewer tools to adapt to changing conditions, making it even more vulnerable to threats like disease or climate change. The vast genetic libraries, stored in the DNA of forest inhabitants, are not just records of evolutionary history but are also keys to future adaptability and survival. Losing them is akin to erasing chapters from the book of life.

Carbon Sequestration:

The term 'carbon sequestration' may sound scientific and detached, but at its heart, it's a lifeline that forests offer in the fight against climate change. Imagine the Earth's forests as vast lungs, breathing in carbon dioxide and offering us clean, oxygenated air. They are nature's solution to a problem we've created, acting as enormous sponges soaking up the carbon emissions we've been recklessly pouring into our atmosphere.

- **Natural Carbon Sinks**: Forests, particularly mature ones, are powerhouses when it comes to capturing carbon. Every leaf, branch, and trunk is a testament to the incredible process of photosynthesis – where trees take in carbon dioxide and, using sunlight, convert it into oxygen and glucose. This glucose, a form of stored energy, represents sequestered carbon. The Amazon Rainforest alone, often termed the 'lungs of the Earth', stores billions of metric tons of carbon and continues to absorb more every year. It's not just the trees; the forest soil, rich with organic matter, also traps a significant amount of carbon. In essence, every inch of a forest is a dedicated warrior against climate change.

- **Releasing Carbon**: The destruction of these carbon vaults results in an immediate and catastrophic release of stored carbon. It's like puncturing those lungs. Whether forests are cleared by burning – releasing carbon directly as CO2 – or left to rot, the once stored carbon finds its way back into our atmosphere. In places like Indonesia, deforestation goes beyond just trees. Draining and clearing peatlands, which can be several meters deep and have accumulated carbon for millennia, releases colossal amounts of greenhouse gases. The aftermath of deforestation isn't just the loss of trees; it's a significant amplification of the very problem trees were mitigating.

- **Loss of Future Carbon Capture**: The tragedy of deforestation isn't limited to the immediate release of stored carbon. It's also about the lost potential. A cleared forest means a loss of future carbon capturing capability. If a forested area is converted into a monoculture plantation or an urban sprawl, its ability to act as a carbon sink is dramatically reduced or entirely nullified. Every tree we lose is a sentinel of carbon capture gone, leaving behind a world that's a little warmer, a little less stable, and facing a future that's increasingly uncertain.

Water Cycles and Soil Erosion

In the intricate web of ecological systems, forests serve as vital nodes, connecting the sky to the ground. They act as environmental stabilizers, ensuring that water cycles function effectively and soils remain fertile and robust. Their role might appear passive at first glance, but forests are active participants in nurturing and sustaining the very foundation of life.

- **Rainfall Regulation**: Forests act as natural sponges, absorbing rainfall and then releasing it back into the atmosphere in a process called transpiration. This perpetual give-and-take creates a localized humidity dome, essentially causing forests to make their own weather. As the water vapor released by trees rises and interacts with the cooler atmospheric layers, it condenses to form clouds. This cloud cover is essential for precipitation. In essence, forests are like colossal water fountains, pumping moisture into the air, aiding in the formation of rain clouds, and influencing weather patterns far beyond their boundaries. There are studies suggesting that the Amazon Rainforest, for instance, plays a role in inducing rainfall in regions as far away as North America.

- **Preventing Soil Erosion**: Forests stand as silent guardians of the soil. The complex network of roots from towering trees, understory vegetation, and ground flora creates a firm mesh, anchoring the soil. This protective grid ensures that, come rain or wind, the topsoil is not easily washed or blown away. Without these root systems, landscapes are vulnerable. When rains hit deforested lands, the topsoil, which harbors essential nutrients, is eroded, eventually finding its way into rivers and streams. This sedimentation not only diminishes the land's agricultural viability but also chokes water bodies, disrupting aquatic ecosystems and reducing water quality for human consumption.

- **Soil Fertility**: Forests are masterful recyclers. Every fallen leaf, every decomposing twig, and even dead fauna contribute to an ongoing organic process. In the quiet beneath the forest canopy, fungi break down this organic matter, converting it to humus, a dark, nutrient-rich component of soil. This organic decomposition ensures that nutrients are continuously cycled back into the soil. When forests are cleared, this cycle is disrupted. The once fertile land, robbed of its organic replenishment, gradually becomes barren. In the absence of this natural composting process, lands lose their productivity, demanding chemical interventions to sustain agriculture, which in the long run can lead to further degradation and ecological imbalance.

Air Quality

Air is the invisible and intangible lifeline, a constant companion that sustains every breath of life on our planet. And while we might take each inhalation for granted, the purity and composition of the air around us are paramount for our well-being. Here, forests emerge as silent custodians, working tirelessly to ensure that the very essence of life, the air we breathe, remains pure and revitalizing.

- **"Lungs of the Planet"**: Drawing a parallel between the function of lungs and forests is not merely poetic but profoundly accurate. Just as our lungs exchange oxygen and carbon dioxide to keep our bodies alive, forests engage in a grander exchange, absorbing vast amounts of carbon dioxide and expelling life-giving oxygen. This respiratory process of trees and plants, known as photosynthesis, is the bedrock of life on Earth. Imagine a single mature leafy tree, which can produce as much oxygen in a season as ten humans inhale in a year. Now extrapolate that to vast expanses like the Amazon, often dubbed the 'Earth's lungs.' This green behemoth stretches over nine countries, housing billions of trees, each contributing to the oxygen reservoir, underscoring the irreplaceable role of forests in our planetary respiratory system.

- **Filtering Pollutants**: But the benevolence of forests doesn't end with oxygen production. They stand as vigilant sentinels, guarding us against the invisible foes that taint our air. Through their leaves and bark, trees absorb a plethora of pollutants. When rainwater passes through the canopy, it washes away these trapped particles, preventing them from being released into the atmosphere. Additionally, forests play a role in trapping particulate matter, which can exacerbate respiratory conditions in humans. By acting as natural air purifiers, forests contribute to overall public health, reducing the burden of diseases related to air pollution.

In essence, forests are not merely passive entities that occupy land. They are dynamic systems, engaged in a ceaseless dance of give-and-take, ensuring that the air around us remains as pristine as nature intended. Every tree felled, every forest patch cleared, is a blow to this delicate balance, making the fight against deforestation not just an environmental concern but a fundamental battle for the very air we breathe.

Socio-Economic Repercussions

Indigenous Communities

Forests have always been more than just a vast expanse of trees and undergrowth; they have been the very essence of life and identity for countless indigenous communities worldwide. To them, every tree, every stream, every rock tells a story, an intertwined tapestry of culture, spirituality, and survival. Yet, as the modern world's bulldozers encroach upon these sanctuaries, we witness not only an environmental tragedy but a heart-wrenching cultural devastation.

- **Cultural Erasure**: Imagine a world where the very cradle of your culture, the bedrock of your beliefs, and the pillars of your community are razed to the ground. For many indigenous peoples, forests are not just sources of sustenance but sanctuaries of spirituality. Within the rustling leaves, they hear the whispers of ancestors; in the babbling brooks, they perceive the songs of spirits; and among ancient trees, they find altars, shrines, and sacred gathering spots. When these forests fall to chainsaws and fires, it's akin to bulldozing cathedrals, temples, and mosques. It's the annihilation of a spiritual realm, obliterating rituals, ceremonies, and oral traditions that have survived for millennia. The loss is immeasurable, transcending material worth, echoing in the void of silenced chants and broken spirits.

- **Forced Displacement**: The violation is further intensified when indigenous peoples are uprooted from their ancestral lands. The land that once provided food, medicine, and shelter becomes inaccessible, replaced by plantations, mines, or barren wastelands. Stripped of their self-sustaining lifestyles, many are forced into unfamiliar urban settings, grappling with the challenges of poverty, unemployment, and cultural alienation. This transition isn't just a change in habitat; it's a profound disconnection from their spiritual roots, an identity crisis that many struggle to reconcile with.

- **Rights and Representation**: One might wonder: How can such transgressions occur in our modern era, replete with international charters, human rights declarations, and environmental conventions? The reality is, while documents like the UN Declaration on the Rights of Indigenous Peoples offer hope, their translation into actionable policies at the national or regional level often falls short. The voices of indigenous communities are muffled under the loud clamor of corporate interests, bureaucratic red tape, and political agendas. Without proper representation in corridors of power and decision-making platforms, these communities often find themselves marginalized, their pleas unheard, their rights trampled.

In understanding the cost of deforestation, we must look beyond just the trees. We must recognize the fading heartbeats of ancient cultures, the silent cries of displaced souls, and the yearning for justice among those who've called these forests home long before the modern world recognized their worth.

Local Economies

In the quest for economic prosperity, nations and corporations often view forests through a myopic lens, perceiving them primarily as resources to be mined, rather than as intricate ecosystems to be nurtured. This short-term approach, while promising immediate financial gains, tends to neglect the nuanced tapestry of local economies, cultures, and environments that have thrived in harmony with these forests for generations.

- **Boom and Bust**: It's a familiar pattern: a company arrives in a forest-rich region, drawn by the allure of untapped resources. The initial phase, often dubbed the 'boom', sees an influx of jobs, capital, and economic activity. Local communities, initially enticed by the promise of better incomes and improved infrastructure, soon realize the transience of this prosperity. Once the timber is logged, the minerals extracted, or the land rendered infertile, the company packs up, leaving behind an ecological wasteland. The subsequent 'bust' phase sees local economies collapsing. The jobs vanish, and the once-bustling towns become ghost towns, with local populations left to grapple with the aftermath of ecological degradation and economic desertion.

- **Loss of Sustainable Livelihoods**: Beyond the direct economic activities linked to forests, countless local communities depend on forests in subtler, sustainable ways. Forests are the hunting grounds, the fishing spots, the herbal gardens, and the spiritual sanctuaries for many. The honey collector relies on the wild bees that nest in tall trees; the herbalist has an intimate knowledge of the forest floor, knowing where to find rare medicinal plants. Fisherfolk depend on clean rivers, which in turn rely on forests to prevent siltation. When forests are razed, these intricate connections are severed. The once self-sufficient communities find themselves in a paradox where they are surrounded by their homeland but are estranged from their traditional means of subsistence. Adapting to alternate livelihoods, often in unfamiliar urban settings, poses a formidable challenge, both culturally and economically.

- **Infrastructure and Development**: The promise of development is a compelling narrative, especially in regions that have historically been marginalized. Roads, dams, and urban centers, seen as symbols of progress, often come at a staggering environmental cost. While a new road might promise better connectivity, it often fragments habitats and opens up pristine forest areas to logging and poaching. Dams, while generating electricity, can submerge vast tracts of forests, displacing both wildlife and local communities. The real question to ponder is: What kind of development are we seeking? If development decimates the very resources and cultural tapestry on which communities have thrived for generations, its long-term viability and desirability remain highly questionable.

Global Implications

In our interconnected world, the devastation of a forest in one part of the globe can have cascading effects, often manifesting in unforeseen ways in distant lands. As boundaries blur in our globalized era, the socio-economic implications of deforestation aren't just a concern for the immediate localities but for nations and societies across continents.

- **Trade Disputes**: Environmental sustainability is no longer a fringe concern; it's mainstream. As nations and consumers become more environmentally conscious, there's mounting scrutiny on products linked to deforestation. Products such as uncertified palm oil, hardwood, or beef from deforested areas have come under the lens. Consequently, nations and blocs have started imposing trade restrictions or tariffs on such goods. For countries whose economies lean heavily on these exports, this can spell economic crises, which can, in turn, ripple into political instability and social turmoil. These trade disputes are not merely about commodities but reflect a larger global conversation about environmental ethics, responsibility, and the nature of sustainable trade in the 21st century.

- **Commodity Prices**: The global market is a delicate web of interdependencies. When large tracts of forest are cleared for monocultures like soy or cattle ranches, it doesn't just impact local ecosystems. It can tip the scales of supply and demand, leading to price fluctuations in global commodity markets. For instance, an excessive clearance of forests for soy production might temporarily flood the market, causing soy prices to dip. This can affect farmers globally, from the American Midwest to the plains of India.

- **Food Security**: Forests, as guardians of water cycles, play an underappreciated role in global food security. By influencing precipitation patterns, they ensure regular and adequate rainfall, a boon for agriculture. Deforestation disrupts these patterns, leading to irregular rainfall, longer droughts, or unseasonal downpours. Such unpredictability can wreak havoc on agricultural cycles, jeopardizing food production. In a world grappling with climate change, where agricultural zones are shifting and traditional farming practices are being challenged, the stability offered by forests becomes even more paramount. Without them, ensuring a stable food supply for an ever-growing global populace becomes a Herculean task.

- **Migration**: Often, the socio-economic fallout from deforestation isn't restricted to dwindling bank balances or faltering industries. It's about uprooted lives. As forests vanish, they take with them livelihoods, ways of life, and environmental stability. Faced with such profound changes, many communities see no option but to migrate in search of better prospects. This migration isn't always local. As environmental and economic refugees, people traverse nations and continents. Such large-scale migrations can strain resources in the regions they move to, potentially sparking geopolitical tensions and challenging the socio-cultural fabric of receiving areas.

The socio-economic repercussions of deforestation are multifaceted and deeply interconnected. Local actions have global consequences, and the costs, often hidden or deferred, are borne by the most vulnerable. It's a stark reminder that the health of our forests is intrinsically linked to the socio-economic well-being of millions worldwide.

Elites, Governments, and Corporate Interests: The Power Dynamics Behind Deforestation

The Role of Elites

Throughout the annals of history, those in positions of power and privilege have often exerted disproportionate influence over natural resources. Forests, being both ecologically significant and economically invaluable, are no exception. In the nexus of power, wealth, and resource control, forests become more than just expanses of green; they are assets, political tools, and often, collateral in the grander schemes of geopolitics and economic dominance.

- **Land Ownership and Control:**

  - **Historical Context**: Colonialism didn't just redraw political boundaries; it reshaped ecological ownership. European colonial powers, in their pursuit of wealth and dominion, often annexed vast tracts of forests, treating them as their private estates. This era saw the commodification of forests, with timber, spices, and other forest resources being exploited for the metropolis. In many cases, land ownership rights were transferred to local elites or colonial settlers, leaving indigenous populations dispossessed. Even after the winds of decolonization swept the world, many of these ownership patterns persisted, laying the groundwork for contemporary conflicts and ecological challenges.

- **Modern Implications**: The echoes of these historical land grabs are audible even today. In many countries, swathes of forested lands are controlled by a handful of families or corporations. While some of these estates might be remnants of colonial-era grants, others are products of modern land acquisition strategies. These forests become sites for luxury resorts, golf courses, or monoculture plantations, serving the interests of the elite while often marginalizing local communities. For the indigenous and forest-dependent populations, this means not only the loss of their homes but also of their cultural heritage, traditional knowledge, and economic sustenance.

- **Influence over Policy:**

  - **Lobbying and Advocacy**: The corridors of power are no strangers to the footsteps of lobbyists representing elite interests. With vast resources at their disposal, many elites employ lobbyists to ensure that forest and land-use policies align with their economic interests. This might manifest as advocacy for softer regulations on logging, rezoning of protected areas, or tax breaks for certain industries. The ripple effects of such lobbying can be profound. Policies that might have protected endangered ecosystems or promoted sustainable land use get diluted, leaving forests vulnerable to unchecked exploitation.

  - **Manipulating Public Perception**: In the age of information, narratives shape realities. Recognizing the power of perception, many elites, directly or indirectly, influence media narratives around deforestation. This could range from promoting the economic benefits of certain forest-depleting projects to sidelining or discrediting environmental activists. Media campaigns might highlight job creation from a new logging project, while downplaying its ecological impact. By controlling the narrative, these power centers can sway public opinion, ensuring a smoother path for their ventures, even if they come at an incalculable ecological cost.

Governments and Policy Failures

Governments, both central and local, wield immense power over the fate of a nation's forests. While they have the tools and authority to enforce sustainable practices, the reality often strays from the ideal. Political pressures, international obligations, economic goals, and internal corruption converge, determining how forests are treated. It's a tangle of priorities where forests, unfortunately, often fall by the wayside.

- **Short-term Gains over Long-term Sustainability:**

    - **Election Cycles**: In democracies around the world, politicians often have an eye on the next election. While this is the nature of representative governance, it can sometimes lead to myopic policy-making. Initiatives that yield quick, tangible results, like infrastructural projects or opening forests for extraction industries, are favored. Such projects can be touted as evidence of "development" and "progress". On the other hand, sustainable initiatives like reforestation or conservation might take years, if not decades, to show results. In the interim, while the benefits are accruing silently, another election might be lost.

- **External Debt and Economic Pressures**: Many nations, especially in the Global South, grapple with enormous external debts. International institutions and creditor nations, while offering financial aid or restructuring debt, often attach strings. These conditionalities might push recipient countries towards "economic reforms" that prioritize rapid industrialization, export-oriented agriculture, or opening up natural resources for exploitation. In this scenario, forests become collateral, sacrificed at the altar of macroeconomic stability.

- **Corruption and Inadequate Regulation:**

- **Porous Borders**: The sheer vastness of some countries makes effective border monitoring a Herculean task. These porous borders become hotspots for illegal logging activities. Rogue loggers, sometimes in collusion with local officials, exploit these gaps, spiriting away precious timber across borders before any alarms are raised. The environmental, social, and economic costs of such unchecked activities are profound, with local ecosystems and communities bearing the brunt of this illicit trade.

- **Judicial Lapses**: Justice delayed is justice denied. In many countries, while environmental regulations might exist on paper, their enforcement is lackluster. Cases against illegal loggers or companies flouting environmental norms might drag on for years in courts. These judicial delays, coupled with the possibility of lenient penalties, embolden violators. Without the fear of swift and stringent retribution, forests continue to be plundered, and the rule of law is rendered ineffective in its role as a protector of the green cover.

Corporate Interests

As entities built upon the foundation of profit maximization, corporations exert a profound influence upon the world's forests. They have the machinery, capital, and reach to access and exploit forest resources on a scale that individual or local entities cannot. However, this power, when unchecked or misused, becomes a formidable force of destruction.

- **The Profit Motive:**

  - **Economic Metrics**: The dominant economic narrative globally has been one of growth. Terms such as GDP growth, stock prices, quarterly profits, and market expansion often dominate corporate boardrooms and policy-making corridors. This unidirectional focus has inherent limitations. For instance, while logging might add to a country's GDP, the environmental costs, which might manifest as floods, droughts, or loss of fertile land due to soil erosion, don't subtract from it. This skewed measurement of "progress" incentivizes extraction over conservation. A forest left standing is economically "unproductive", but one that's logged adds to economic "growth". This paradox is at the heart of rampant deforestation.

  - **Externalizing Costs**: One of the classic strategies employed by many corporations globally is the externalization of costs. In simple terms, it means that while the profits are privatized, the costs, especially the environmental and social ones, are socialized. A corporation might extract timber from a forest and sell it for substantial profit. However, the loss of that forest might lead to local climatic changes, forcing a farming community to deal with erratic rainfall. The health costs from polluted air, the loss of livelihood for indigenous communities, or the cost of rebuilding after intensified natural disasters due to ecological imbalance, are borne by communities and governments, not the corporations. This displacement of responsibility ensures that their balance sheets remain green, even if the forests do not.

- **Lack of Transparency in Supply Chains:**

  - **Complex Web**: The vast, sprawling supply chains of today's corporations can resemble a labyrinthine web. A single product, like a smartphone or a chocolate bar, may have its roots in numerous countries, involving hundreds of suppliers. The intricacies of this supply web make it easy for unethical practices to be buried deep within. For instance, a product using palm oil might be several steps removed from the deforestation caused by a supplier's supplier, making accountability elusive.

  - **Consumer Disconnect**: For the ordinary consumer, understanding these multi-layered supply chains becomes a Herculean task. The journey of a wooden table, from a forest to a furniture showroom, might involve illegal logging, multiple intermediaries, and several stages of processing and transportation. With each stage, the product's connection to deforestation becomes fainter in the consumer's mind, making conscientious purchasing decisions difficult.

- **Greenwashing:**

  - **Advertising Over Action**: In an era where environmental consciousness is gaining momentum, corporations are keen to present themselves as eco-friendly. However, not infrequently, the reality falls short of the glossy advertisements. This "greenwashing" phenomenon sees companies spending significantly on marketing their supposed "green" credentials – often in stark contrast to the actual ecological impact of their operations. A company might run a high-profile campaign about planting thousands of trees, diverting attention from the millions it might be responsible for felling.

  - **Certification Misuse**: Third-party certifications have emerged as tools for consumers to identify eco-friendly products. Yet, the waters are muddied when corporations exert influence over these certification bodies or exploit loopholes in the certification criteria. Terms like "sustainably sourced" or "environment-friendly" can sometimes be based on weak standards or ambiguous definitions. The result? Consumers, trying to make ethical choices, are misled by a false sense of assurance.

This in-depth exploration highlights the interplay of power, politics, and profit in shaping the fate of the world's forests. The tapestry of interests is intricate, but understanding it is crucial to formulating solutions to the deforestation crisis.

Deforestation Hotspots

The Amazon

Often dubbed the "Earth's Green Lung", the Amazon Rainforest is a living testament to nature's grandeur and complexity. It boasts an unrivaled biodiversity, with millions of species of flora and fauna, many of which remain undiscovered. The Amazon plays a vital role in global weather patterns, water cycles, and is a significant carbon sink, absorbing vast amounts of carbon dioxide. Yet, the very magnitude of the Amazon also makes it a hotspot for human exploitation.

The labyrinthine rivers, verdant canopy, and the symphony of animal calls mask an underlying tension. Every acre cleared in the Amazon represents not just the loss of potential medicines, undiscovered species, or carbon absorption capacity but a blow to the indigenous communities that call the rainforest home.

- **Case Study: The Kayapó Tribe:**

  - **Located in Brazil**: The Kayapó Tribe's territory sprawls across an area the size of Austria in northern Brazil. A community deeply intertwined with its environment, the Kayapó have a profound understanding of the forest's rhythms and nuances. Their traditions, stories, and rituals echo the whispers of the forest, and they have become emblematic of the indigenous fight against deforestation.

  - **Resistance against Encroachment**: For the Kayapó, the forest isn't just a habitat; it's an ancestral land steeped in memories, legends, and spirits. The intrusion of illegal loggers, miners, and cattle ranchers isn't merely an economic issue but an existential threat. They've witnessed firsthand the scars left behind by logging: muddied rivers, silenced animal calls, and an unsettling stillness.

Their resistance has been a blend of traditional knowledge and modern tools. By partnering with NGOs, they've harnessed satellite technology to keep a vigilant eye over their vast territories. These satellite images often act as evidence of illegal activities, which the Kayapó present in regional and national meetings, demanding action.

- **Preserving Heritage and Ecosystem**: Beyond the lush canopy, the Amazon for the Kayapó is a repository of their ancestors' tales, a playground where generations learned to hunt, fish, and respect nature. Every tree felled or river polluted erases pages from their rich cultural tapestry.

Moreover, the tribe understands the ecological web where every element, from the towering Brazil nut trees to the stealthy jaguars, plays a part. The harpy eagle, with its impressive wingspan, is not just a magnificent bird but a part of the forest's soul, and its declining numbers are a barometer of the health of the ecosystem.

Through their unwavering commitment, the Kayapó Tribe offers the world a lesson in stewardship, illustrating that the battle against deforestation is not just about trees but the very essence of life and heritage.

Southeast Asian Rainforests

The rainforests of Southeast Asia, draped in a rich tapestry of biodiversity, are among the oldest on Earth. Having evolved over millions of years, these rainforests are a mesmerizing blend of dense foliage, roaring rivers, and a myriad of life forms that range from the invisible to the gigantic. Each layer of the forest, from the dark understory to the sun-kissed canopy, tells a unique tale of coexistence and symbiosis.

However, the modern narrative of these rainforests is fraught with machinery roars, land clearings, and a race to tap into the 'green gold' - palm oil. Southeast Asia, notably Indonesia and Malaysia, has become the global epicenter for palm oil production. And while palm oil is found in everything from lipsticks to chocolates and is hailed for its efficiency as a crop, the environmental costs are staggering.

- **Case Study: The Orangutan:**

    - **The "Man of the Forest"**: The orangutan, whose name in the Malay language translates to "man of the forest," is an apt reflection of its deep connection with the rainforest habitat. With their expressive eyes and almost human-like demeanor, orangutans are not just a species; they're a symbol of the rainforest's soul. Their daily life, swinging from trees, foraging fruits, and building nests, is a testament to the intricate relationship between a species and its environment.

    - **Borneo and Sumatra: Ground Zero**: The islands of Borneo and Sumatra, known for their lush landscapes and rich biodiversity, are the last bastions for the orangutans. But as palm oil plantations burgeon, forests are razed, fragmenting the orangutan's habitat. This fragmentation doesn't just mean loss of home; it means difficulty in finding food, increased vulnerability to predators, and challenges in mating.

Moreover, as orangutans venture out of the forests into plantations or local villages in search of food, they are often met with hostility. Many are killed as pests, while others fall victim to pet trade or are left injured and traumatized.

- **The Broader Ecosystem Impact**: While the orangutan's plight is poignant, it's reflective of the larger ecological crisis. For every orangutan lost, countless other species, from insects and birds to plants and fungi, face similar existential threats. The rich symphony of the rainforest is slowly being replaced by a monotonous hum of palm trees.

- **Conservation: A Ray of Hope**: Several NGOs, conservationists, and even certain palm oil companies have initiated efforts to rehabilitate injured orangutans and reintroduce them into the wild. Sanctuaries have sprung up, aiming to provide a temporary home for these displaced individuals. However, true success lies not just in saving individual orangutans but in a paradigm shift in how we perceive and utilize forests. Only by addressing the insatiable demand for palm oil and promoting sustainable farming can the orangutan – and the myriad of life forms in the rainforest – truly thrive.

Central African Forests

Stretching across multiple nations, the rainforests of Central Africa stand as vast emerald blankets teeming with life. These forests, dense with greenery, represent a world that seems largely untouched by modern civilization, with its rivers, waterfalls, and varied terrains hosting a cacophony of sounds, from bird calls to insect hums.

But beneath this pristine image lies a reality of exploitation and endangerment. The rich timber resources of these forests have become a lucrative attraction for both local and international logging companies. Additionally, beneath the forest floor, the land is rich in minerals, leading to extensive mining operations. As if these were not enough, the forests also bear the brunt of the bushmeat trade, where exotic animals are hunted to be sold in urban markets or exported.

- **Case Study: The Mbuti Pygmies of the Congo:**

  - **Living Libraries of the Forest**: The Mbuti Pygmies, one of the indigenous tribes of the Ituri Rainforest, have lived harmoniously with nature for centuries. Their songs, stories, and daily routines are deeply woven into the tapestry of the forest. Their footprint is light, only taking from the forest what they need and ensuring that they give back in their own ways.

    Their nomadic lifestyle, built around the seasons and animal movements, showcases an intricate knowledge of the forest's rhythms. From identifying medicinal plants to tracking elusive game, the Mbuti have a profound understanding of their surroundings, making them living libraries of forest wisdom.

- **Clash of Traditional and Modern**: However, the modern world is steadily encroaching upon their ancestral lands. Large swathes of the Ituri Rainforest are being earmarked for logging or transformed into national parks. While the latter might seem like a conservation effort, it restricts the Mbuti from practicing their traditional hunting and gathering, pushing them to the fringes and often into conflict with park authorities.

  Moreover, the regions that are open to them are increasingly impacted by external activities. Logging not only destroys their home but disrupts the delicate ecological balance, affecting animal populations and plant growth. Similarly, the presence of miners seeking gold or coltan (used in mobile phones and electronics) introduces alcohol, drugs, and diseases into the Mbuti communities, further eroding their traditional way of life.

- **A Partnership for Conservation**: Despite the challenges they face, the Mbuti's deep-rooted connection to the forest makes them invaluable allies in conservation efforts. Recognizing their unique knowledge and understanding of the forest can pave the way for collaborative conservation initiatives. By integrating the Mbuti's traditional knowledge with modern conservation techniques, a more holistic approach to preserving the Ituri Rainforest can be established.

Yet, time is of the essence. Every day that their voice is not integrated into the broader conversation about the forest's future is a day closer to losing not just an invaluable human culture but also the intricate ecological balance of one of the world's most magnificent rainforests.

Other Notable Regions

From the towering sequoias of California to the sprawling eucalyptus groves of Australia, forests make up some of the most majestic landscapes on our planet. Yet, irrespective of their geographical location or the unique flora and fauna they house, these forests face threats that often mirror each other - threats born out of human ambition, economic pursuits, and often, sheer ignorance about the balance of nature.

- **Case Study: The Caribou in the North American Boreal Forests:**

  - **A Glimpse into the Boreal World**: The boreal forest, often referred to as the "Earth's green crown," is a vast expanse of wilderness, characterized by its coniferous trees, wetlands, and countless lakes. This seemingly endless stretch of green represents one of the largest intact forest ecosystems on Earth. The quiet serenity is occasionally interrupted by the calls of its many inhabitants, from migratory birds to large mammals.

    The forest undergoes dramatic changes with the seasons. Summers, though brief, bring forth a burst of life, while winters transform the landscape into a snowy wonderland, punctuated by the Northern Lights' ethereal glow. But this pristine beauty masks the underlying threats that the forest faces.

- **The Caribou's Plight**: The woodland caribou, with its majestic antlers and adaptive nature, has long been a symbol of the wild, untamed beauty of the boreal forests. These creatures have evolved over millennia to thrive in the unique conditions of the boreal regions. They have specially adapted hooves that allow them to traverse deep snow and to dig for the lichen that forms their primary diet during the long winter months.

However, the serene world of the caribou is being steadily intruded upon. Logging trucks, noisy oil drilling operations, and bright mining sites have begun to scar the vast landscape. The disturbances caused by these activities are not just physical. They disrupt the caribou's migration patterns, make them more vulnerable to predators, and, crucially, diminish their food sources. Mature forests, rich in lichen, are being replaced by younger forests that do not offer the same sustenance.

- **Colliding Interests**: The debate around conserving the caribou's habitat is multi-faceted. On one side, there's the undeniable ecological value of preserving one of the world's largest intact forests and the species that call it home. On the other, there are the economic interests, with the boreal forests sitting atop vast reserves of oil, minerals, and timber. These resources offer employment, contribute to the GDP, and are vital for many industries.

Yet, the middle ground remains elusive. Some suggest sustainable logging and extraction methods, while others advocate for complete bans in critical habitats. Indigenous communities, who have lived in harmony with these forests for centuries, offer valuable insights into coexistence, often drawing from a rich history of sustainable practices.

As we move forward, the fate of the boreal forest and its iconic caribou hangs in the balance, serving as a potent reminder of the intricate web of life and the consequences of our choices.

These case studies offer a microcosmic view into the larger tragedy unfolding in our world's forests. The intertwined destinies of indigenous communities, wildlife, and ecosystems underline the urgency of addressing deforestation in these hotspots.

Climate Change and Deforestation

Feedback Loops

In the delicate equilibrium of nature, forests and climate share a symbiotic relationship, with each influencing the health and state of the other. Disrupting this balance sets off a chain reaction, and understanding this intricate interplay is pivotal to grasping the global environmental crisis at hand.

- **Forests as Carbon Sinks**: Forests, often visualized as the green lungs of our planet, are more than just passive entities absorbing carbon dioxide. Their vast canopies, intricate root systems, and rich soil form a complex storage mechanism. These systems not only draw down carbon dioxide during photosynthesis but also store carbon in various forms, including in the very wood and leaves of the trees, and in the soil as organic matter.

- However, when forests are cleared – whether due to logging or to make way for agriculture – the stored carbon gets released. In fact, deforestation is responsible for about 10% of global carbon emissions. What's even more distressing is that once cleared, the potential of these areas to act as future carbon sinks is significantly reduced or entirely lost, especially if they transform into non-forest uses.

- **Warming and Forest Health**: Rising global temperatures, often felt as prolonged heatwaves, directly stress forests. Just like other living organisms, trees have temperature and moisture levels they prefer. With changing climates, many trees experience water stress, reducing their growth rates and making them vulnerable to pests and diseases.

- The increased vulnerability due to warming has another cascading effect: forest fires. While forest fires are natural occurrences and play a role in some ecosystems, the increasing frequency and intensity of these fires are concerning. Intense fires not only decimate wildlife habitats but leave behind charred lands that take years to recover.

- **Altered Rainfall Patterns**: Forests have an intrinsic relationship with water. Through a process called transpiration, trees release water vapor from their leaves, which then forms clouds and returns as rainfall. But with extensive deforestation, this water recycling system gets disrupted.

- Regions that once relied on forests for regular rainfall find themselves facing unpredictable weather patterns. Some areas, once lush and green, turn arid and face prolonged droughts, directly impacting agriculture and freshwater availability. Conversely, without forests to act as buffers, some areas experience excessive rainfall, causing rivers to overflow and leading to devastating floods.

- **Biodiversity and Climate Resilience**: Diverse ecosystems are robust ecosystems. Each species in a forest, from the tiniest insect to the largest mammal, plays a specific role. Some aid in pollination, some in decomposition, and some even in soil aeration. When forests are cleared, this complex web of life unravels.

As species die off due to habitat loss, the forest loses its natural defense mechanisms. This loss of biodiversity weakens the forest's ability to recover from natural disasters or disease outbreaks. In the context of climate change, a biodiverse forest stands a better chance at adapting to changing conditions, whether it's shifting weather patterns or the introduction of new pests. In essence, biodiversity is the shield against the uncertainties of a changing climate.

Carbon Taxes/Fines and the Role of Forests in Carbon Trading

In the global quest to curb carbon emissions and battle climate change, economic and market-based instruments like carbon trading and carbon taxes have gained prominence. Forests, with their innate capacity to sequester vast amounts of carbon, are inextricably intertwined in these financial mechanisms. However, as with any large-scale economic solution, its efficacy depends on nuanced understanding, meticulous planning, and unyielding commitment.

- **Carbon Offsets and REDD**: The UN's REDD program presents a dual advantage – it provides developing countries with an incentive to conserve forests while allowing industrialized nations or corporations to offset their carbon footprint. However, beneath this seemingly win-win situation lie a plethora of challenges:

  - **Quantification Issues:** Measuring the exact amount of carbon stored in forests is complex. Factors like forest type, maturity, and health play a role, leading to potential discrepancies in the number of credits generated and their real-world impact.

- **Socio-Economic Implications:** By commercializing forests in the form of carbon credits, there's a risk of sidelining the rights and needs of indigenous communities. There's also the concern that this could lead to 'carbon colonialism,' where rich nations or corporations control the forest resources of poorer nations without substantial on-ground benefits for local populations.

- **Leakage Concerns:** While a forest might be conserved in one region due to REDD credits, logging or deforestation could simply shift to another, unmonitored region.

- **Stricter Fines and Taxes**: Merely acknowledging the environmental repercussions of deforestation is not enough; tangible financial deterrents are necessary to catalyze real change.

  - **Holding Corporations Accountable**: While many corporations publicly endorse sustainable practices, there's a chasm between words and actions. Imposing stiff fines, especially when backed by satellite imagery and on-ground audits, can deter environmentally harmful activities. This method has its roots in the 'polluter pays' principle, where entities that cause environmental damage are held financially responsible.

  - **Taxing Unsustainable Practices**: A shift in the economic landscape, where products linked to deforestation are taxed higher, can create a ripple effect. It can prompt corporations to rethink sourcing strategies and might even lead to innovations in sustainable product development. However, for such a system to be impactful, international cooperation is paramount. An isolated tax in one country could merely push the trade to another region with more lenient regulations.

- **Transparency and Implementation**: The success of any large-scale program hinges on its transparent implementation. In the realm of carbon trading and taxes:

  - **Third-party Audits:** Independent assessments, free from governmental or corporate influence, can ensure that conservation efforts funded by carbon trading or taxes are genuine and effective.

  - **Stakeholder Involvement:** Including indigenous communities, local NGOs, and environmental experts in planning and monitoring can lend credibility and holistic effectiveness to these initiatives.

  - **International Oversight:** Given the transboundary nature of many corporations and the global implications of deforestation, international bodies can play a pivotal role in monitoring, verification, and ensuring that the funds are channeled appropriately.

In the context of the existential threat posed by climate change, deforestation stands as both a contributing factor and a missed mitigation opportunity. Striking the right balance between economic growth and conservation, underpinned by stringent, transparent policies, is crucial to break the vicious cycle of deforestation and climate change.

Psychological and Health Impacts

Forest Bathing and Mental Health

The nexus between nature and mental well-being has always been woven into the tapestry of human existence. Stories, poems, and ancient medical practices frequently alluded to the rejuvenating properties of nature. In our modern, hyper-connected world, where concrete jungles often dwarf natural ones, there is a resurging need to rediscover and harness the healing powers of forests.

- **Origins of Forest Bathing**: The term 'Shinrin-yoku' beautifully encapsulates the Japanese philosophy that reveres nature as a source of emotional and physical healing. The phrase doesn't merely signify a walk in the woods; it invites individuals to commune with the forest. To listen to the rustle of leaves, feel the texture of bark, inhale the aroma of moss, and witness the kaleidoscope of life that forests teem with.

  - **Cultural Context**: In Japan, where urban life can be particularly hectic, the forest is seen as a sanctuary. Traditional tea ceremonies, Zen gardens, and even certain martial arts practices are deeply intertwined with nature, hinting at the nation's inherent recognition of nature's significance.

  - **Prescriptive Nature**: Recognizing the profound effects of forest immersion, Japanese agencies designated specific forests as therapeutic, and some doctors began incorporating forest therapy into their holistic health recommendations.

- **Scientific Backing**: Modern science offers empirical validation to what ancient wisdom and intuition have always hinted at: forests are good for our well-being.

  - **Neurological Impact**: MRI scans and EEG studies have shown that forest environments can induce changes in the brain, promoting relaxation and enhancing creative thinking.

  - **Immune System Boost**: Beyond mental well-being, exposure to forests has been linked to a bolstered immune system, likely due to the inhalation of beneficial phytoncides and reduced stress levels.

  - **Therapeutic Applications**: Some therapists incorporate forest bathing into treatment plans for individuals suffering from chronic depression, PTSD, and certain addictive behaviors, attesting to its broad therapeutic potential.

- **Nature-Deficit Disorder**: As urbanization surges and screens become dominant in our lives, our disconnect from nature deepens. This chasm has profound repercussions, especially for the younger generations.

  - **Child Development**: Children who don't experience nature miss out on its cognitive, emotional, and social benefits. Playing in natural settings fosters creativity, enhances problem-solving skills, and promotes better social interaction.

  - **Physical Health Implications**: Beyond psychological costs, a lack of interaction with nature also correlates with certain physical health issues, such as obesity, myopia, and vitamin D deficiency.

- **Rekindling the Bond**: Addressing nature-deficit disorder isn't just about frequent forest visits. It also involves integrating nature into urban design, promoting community gardens, ensuring school curricula incorporate outdoor learning, and encouraging families to adopt nature-oriented lifestyles.

Loss of Medical Cures

Forests, with their rich tapestry of life, have served as the world's ancient apothecaries. From tribal shamans to modern pharmacologists, the quest for healing often leads back to the heart of the forest. Yet, as chainsaws and bulldozers penetrate deeper into these green sanctuaries, the echoes of lost cures grow louder.

- **Biodiversity and Pharmacology**: The symbiotic relationships, evolutionary pressures, and sheer diversity within forests have fostered a hotbed of biochemical innovation among plants and animals. These biochemical compounds, honed over millennia, have been a treasure trove for medical researchers.

  - **Nature's Laboratory**: Many of the compounds found in plants are the result of evolutionary pressures—natural defenses against herbivores, infections, or rival plants. These compounds, when studied, can often be harnessed for their potent therapeutic effects on humans.

  - **Potential vs. Reality**: While the number of studied plants remains minimal, the few that have been researched have already yielded significant results. Aspirin (from willow bark), quinine (from the cinchona tree), and morphine (from the opium poppy) are just a few examples of medicines that originated from plant-based compounds.

- **The Tip of the Iceberg**: As pharmaceutical research becomes increasingly sophisticated, the demand for novel compounds grows. Forests, particularly the yet unexplored or understudied regions, hold promises of groundbreaking medical discoveries.

- **Spotlight: The Rosy Periwinkle**: This seemingly inconspicuous plant, with its delicate pink flowers, exemplifies the boundless potential forests harbor. Its story underscores the profound implications of forest conservation on global health.

  - **Cultural Context**: The indigenous communities in Madagascar used the rosy periwinkle for treating various ailments long before its cancer-fighting properties were recognized by the global medical community.

  - **Economic Implications**: The success of vincristine and vinblastine not only revolutionized leukemia treatment but also turned into a multi-billion dollar industry. It brings to light the potential economic value of conserving forests and responsibly harnessing their resources.

  - **Beyond the Periwinkle**: Madagascar's forests, like many other biodiversity hotspots, face severe deforestation threats. The loss of such habitats doesn't just mean the extinction of known species but also countless undiscovered ones, each potentially holding the key to medical revolutions.

The perilous trajectory of deforestation isn't just an ecological tragedy; it is a potential health catastrophe. As forests fall silent, the hope for novel cures becomes ever more elusive. The need of the hour is to recognize forests not just as timber reserves but as invaluable vaults of biodiversity and medical potential.

The intricate relationship humans have with forests extends beyond the tangible. It's embedded in our psyche, our well-being, and our health. As forests disappear, the repercussions are not just ecological but also deeply personal, affecting our mental health, physical well-being, and potential future discoveries that could reshape medicine. This understanding underscores the importance of conservation not just for the planet but also for the very essence of human well-being.

Modern Industries and Deforestation

Pharmaceuticals

The pharmaceutical realm, a blend of modern science and nature's ancient bounties, is rooted deeply in forests, Earth's age-old medicine chests. While these woodlands have consistently offered their treasures to both scientists and age-old healers, the swift ascendancy of the pharmaceutical sector, coupled with the allure of hidden curatives, has thrust these ecosystems into a delicate equipoise.

- **Bioprospecting**: Venturing deep into forested terrains, researchers quest for plants, fungi, and sometimes even animal substances that could metamorphose into groundbreaking drugs. Yet, this pursuit doesn't come without repercussions. Although bioprospecting should ideally respect its natural environment, commercial pressures sometimes tilt the scales towards a more intrusive exploration, disrupting the delicate ecological balance. Often, it's the indigenous communities, well-versed in their local ecology, that step in as guides. Their age-old wisdom, however, demands respect, not just tokenistic gestures.

- **Intellectual Property Controversies**: The intellectual rights associated with nature's remedies are multifaceted. Central to this discourse is an ethical conundrum: To whom does knowledge, nurtured across eons, truly belong? And how does one bestow rightful recognition or compensation to entire communities for insights passed down through generations?

Some forward-thinking pharmaceutical entities have acknowledged this and have embarked on models that channelize a fraction of the profits from these traditional knowledge-derived drugs back to their original custodians.

- **Sustainable Harvesting vs. Over-Exploitation**: Treading the nuanced line between sustainable harvesting and over-exploitation becomes even more intricate under the influence of commercial pursuits. A sudden surge in demand for a newly discovered plant compound can catalyze rampant harvesting, jeopardizing the very ecosystems these plants belong to. In response, certain initiatives have looked towards cultivating these medicinal plants, attempting to strike a balance between demand and conservation.

- **Conservation Opportunities**: Indeed, the interplay between forests and the pharmaceutical industry need not be adversarial. Some visionary companies have championed the establishment of nature reserves, thus ensuring both the preservation of medicinal plant diversity and a sustainable resource repository. By shedding light on the forest origins of many modern medicines, the industry can kindle a broader appreciation for these vital ecosystems, fostering a symbiotic relationship where both conservation and commerce flourish in tandem.

Mining and Drilling:

The inexorable march of industrialization, underpinned by the modern world's voracious appetite for minerals and energy, invariably comes into conflict with the planet's green bastions.

Forests, these intricate networks of life, are often the collateral damage in humanity's quest for underground riches.

- **Clearance and Infrastructure**: Before the first echoes of machinery sound in the forest, the initial act is one of clearing. These aren't just mere acts of removing trees; they symbolize the displacement of myriad life forms that called these places home. It's not merely the expanse of the mine itself; the infrastructure that supports such operations extends like tentacles into the forest. Roads, perhaps seen as benign conduits for transportation, in reality, act as barriers, impeding the movement of animals, fragmenting habitats, and opening the floodgates for other forms of exploitation. The once-secluded territories become accessible, not just to the miners, but to everyone from loggers to poachers.

- **Environmental Contamination**: If the act of clearing forests is a visible scar, the contamination from mining is an insidious poison that creeps into the very veins of the ecosystem. Consider gold mining. The allure of this precious metal has often been tainted by the use of mercury, a potent neurotoxin. This toxic element doesn't just remain confined to the mine; it meanders into rivers, enters the food chain, and wreaks havoc on aquatic life and the communities that rely on these waterways. It's a legacy of contamination that outlasts the life of the mine itself.

- **Fossil Fuel Extraction**: Nowhere is the irony of deforestation more striking than in the extraction of fossil fuels. These regions, like the Amazon, already serve as the planet's bulwarks against climate change. Yet, they are punctured and drained of oil and natural gas, which, when burned, release vast amounts of CO2. In essence, we're trading short-term energy gains for long-term climate stability, compromising not only the health of the planet but the very air we breathe.

- **Indigenous Land Rights and Conflicts**: Amidst the cacophony of machinery and the discourse on economic progress, the voices of the forest's original custodians often get drowned. For indigenous communities, forests aren't just resource reservoirs but realms of ancestry, culture, and spirituality. The incursion of mining entities isn't merely a business venture; it's an intrusion into sacred spaces. Promises of economic prosperity by extractive industries often contrast starkly with the ground realities these communities face: forced evictions, cultural erosion, and a sense of alienation in their own lands. The very essence of sustainable living, honed over centuries, stands challenged by industries that measure progress in quarterly financial reports.

As the global demand for medicines, minerals, and energy continues to grow, the pressure on forests intensifies. Striking a balance between development and conservation requires rethinking industry practices, enforcing stricter regulations, and, most importantly, recognizing the intrinsic value of forests beyond their exploitable resources.

The Role of Financial Institutions

Banking and Investments

Financial behemoths, with their intricate web of capital flows and investments, are sometimes overlooked players in the deforestation narrative. Yet, their influence, underlined by the decisions they make about where to place their funds, can have repercussions that echo through forests worldwide.

- **Project Financing**: Imagine the scale of infrastructure projects that reshape landscapes—these are not small undertakings. The construction of highways that bifurcate dense forests, expansive agricultural fields that replace biodiverse habitats, or sprawling mines that hollow out the earth—all these projects command significant financial resources. The coffers of multinational banks and global investment firms are often the source of this capital. The sheer act of approving or denying funds becomes an implicit endorsement of the project's environmental implications. While a project's feasibility is often evaluated on economic terms, the ecological costs, such as habitat loss or potential species extinction, should be intrinsic to funding decisions.

- **Indirect Contributions**: The financial world's complexity is such that a bank's involvement in deforestation might not always be overt. Consider the convoluted corporate structures where a bank provides loans or invests in a company. This company, on the surface, might not be involved in deforestation. However, a deeper dive into its affiliates, subsidiaries, or business partners could reveal ties to industries that actively harm forests. Thus, financial institutions can inadvertently find themselves complicit in the degradation of ecosystems.

- **Risk Analysis**: Risk, in financial parlance, often revolves around market dynamics, geopolitics, or economic metrics. Yet, the environment, crucial as it is, remains an oft-underrepresented factor in risk assessments. While a project might promise lucrative returns, what of the long-term consequences? The loss of a forest might lead to local climate anomalies, affecting agriculture and communities. Or the loss of biodiversity might mean the disappearance of potential medicinal plants. Such environmental risks need to be integrated into the very algorithms and models that dictate investment strategies.

- **Shareholder Pressures**: The drumbeat of shareholder expectations provides a relentless soundtrack to the operations of investment firms and banks. Every quarter, the spotlight is on returns, dividends, and growth. This relentless focus on the short term, driven by shareholder demands, can sometimes eclipse broader, holistic visions of investment. An investment that safeguards forests, supports sustainable industries, and fosters community development might not yield immediate returns but holds the promise of a stable, long-term gain. Financial institutions must juggle these pressures while also considering their role as stewards of a sustainable future.

Divestment Movements:

The world of finance is not just about cold numbers; it's a reflection of society's values and priorities. As the ecological implications of investments come under the scanner, divestment movements have emerged as powerful tools, challenging the traditional paradigms of finance. These movements, driven by societal actors from students to celebrities, are not just about pulling out funds. They symbolize a collective call for a more responsible, sustainable financial landscape.

- **Student-Led Movements**: Picture this: energetic university campuses, the epicenters of thought and innovation, bubbling with passionate students advocating for a cleaner planet. University endowments, repositories of vast wealth, have historically invested in a diversified portfolio, sometimes including industries detrimental to the environment. Recognizing this, student-led movements have risen to prominence, challenging the very institutions that educate them. Campaigns at prestigious universities like Harvard and Yale have shone a spotlight on the moral incongruities of profiting from industries that jeopardize our planet's future. These movements, driven by informed debates, peaceful protests, and strategic lobbying, have pressured universities to re-evaluate their investment priorities.

- **Public Figures and Divestment**: The weight of a public figure's voice cannot be underestimated in shaping public opinion. When a celebrity or an influential investor speaks out, it amplifies the message manifold. Icons like Warren Buffett or Leonardo DiCaprio, by endorsing divestment, not only inspire their vast followers but also make boardrooms sit up and take notice. Their advocacy often encourages rigorous debate on investment ethics and nudges financial institutions towards introspection.

- **Impact of Divestment**: On the surface, divestment might seem like a symbolic gesture. However, its ripple effects are far-reaching. When a prominent institution divests, it sends shockwaves through the financial community, signaling a changing tide of public opinion. Over time, as more institutions join the chorus and divest from environmentally harmful industries, it can impact the very financial lifeline of these sectors. Reduced investments can translate to reduced operational capacities for industries linked to deforestation, potentially slowing down their activities.

- **Green Investment Opportunities**: Every action has a reaction. As funds are pulled from ecologically damaging ventures, where do they flow? The vacuum created by divestment is increasingly being filled by sustainable investment opportunities. The financial world is waking up to the lucrative prospects of green bonds, which finance projects with environmental benefits, or the appeal of investing in sustainable agriculture that harmonizes with nature rather than exploiting it. Moreover, the renewable energy sector, with its promise of combating climate change, is seeing a surge in investments. These trends are more than just fleeting financial fads; they represent a paradigm shift in how the world views investments—where returns are not just monetary but also ecological.

The financial world, with its immense influence on global economic trends, has a pivotal role to play in the future of the world's forests. As public awareness grows and priorities shift, there's hope that the nexus between money and deforestation can be broken, channeling the power of finance towards a greener, more sustainable future.

Urbanization and Forests

Urban Forests

In an era where urbanization often means endless expanses of steel, glass, and concrete, the concept of urban forests emerges as a vital counterbalance. These green oases, pockets of nature amidst urban sprawl, represent not just aesthetic choices but strategic decisions to enhance the livability and ecological health of cities.

- **Benefits:**

  - **Mental Well-being**: Imagine taking a break from the monotony of your office desk and strolling through a lush green park, or reading a book under the canopy of trees on a sunny day. The serenity and connection to nature offered by urban forests are invaluable for mental health. In the hustle and bustle of city life, these spaces provide a haven of calm and tranquility. They have been found to reduce feelings of anxiety, depression, and fatigue. Moreover, the aesthetic beauty of urban forests, with their seasonal color changes, blossoming flowers, and the soothing sounds of birdsong, enriches the urban experience, promoting mindfulness and offering sensory delights.

  - **Air Purification**: With urbanization often comes the challenge of pollution. Cars, industries, and daily human activities release a plethora of pollutants into the air. Here's where urban forests play the role of unsung heroes. Trees, with their vast leafy expanses, act as natural filters, trapping particulate matter and absorbing pollutants like carbon monoxide, sulfur dioxide, and nitrogen dioxide. The process of photosynthesis also means that these urban green spaces are constantly absorbing carbon dioxide and releasing fresh oxygen, making city air more breathable. Moreover, during scorching summer days, the cooling effect provided by trees through shade and transpiration is invaluable, combating the heat island effect that many cities experience.

- **Biodiversity Hubs**: Often, when we think of biodiversity, sprawling national parks or untouched wilderness areas come to mind. But urban forests, if nurtured, can be teeming with life. They can be home to an array of bird species, from common sparrows to migratory birds seeking temporary refuge. Butterflies, bees, and other insects find nourishment in the flora of these green spaces. Even mammals like squirrels or raccoons might make an appearance, much to the delight of urban dwellers. Moreover, these forests are often repositories of diverse plant species, some ornamental, others native, creating layers of understory, canopy, and ground cover. This diversity not only enriches the ecological fabric of cities but also educates urbanites about the wonders of nature right at their doorstep.

- **Challenges:**

- **Land Scarcity**: In bustling cities, every square foot of land is seen not just as space, but as potential – potential for new homes, businesses, or infrastructure. The pace of urban development, often fueled by migration and population growth, means that land becomes an increasingly scarce and valuable commodity. Against this backdrop, the choice to earmark areas solely for the purpose of green space is not merely a design choice, but a statement of priorities. Every patch of land set aside for an urban forest represents a potential building or commercial space forgone. Moreover, as cities grapple with housing shortages and seek to maximize utility from available land, urban forests can be viewed by some stakeholders as 'wasted' or 'underutilized' space. This perspective underscores the challenge of balancing immediate economic interests against long-term environmental and societal benefits.

- **Maintenance**: Beyond the initial hurdle of establishing an urban forest is the ongoing task of nurturing it. Unlike wild forests, urban ones don't entirely sustain themselves. They exist in a delicate balance, continually influenced by their surroundings. Pollution, especially in industrialized cities, poses a significant threat. Leaves covered in dust or smog cannot photosynthesize efficiently, affecting the health of the trees. Vehicular emissions can lead to soil acidification, which, in turn, impacts the nutrient absorption capacity of tree roots. Water, the lifeblood of any forest, presents its challenges in an urban setting. With concrete surfaces dominating urban landscapes, natural groundwater recharge is compromised, often leading to water shortages. Urban forests, therefore, rely on consistent human-led interventions to ensure they receive adequate water. Furthermore, the influx of visitors means litter and waste, which necessitate regular cleaning drives. Also, pests and diseases, if not monitored and managed, can rapidly degrade the health of these forests.

However, beyond these challenges lies the essence of why urban forests are worth the effort. They stand as testaments to a city's commitment to the environment, to the well-being of its residents, and to a vision of development that harmoniously coexists with nature.

Urban Heat Island (UHI) Effect

An omnipresent phenomenon in rapidly urbanizing landscapes, the Urban Heat Island effect, is a direct testament to how human interventions can alter local climatic patterns. As cities expand and skyscrapers touch the clouds, the warmth that envelopes urban areas starkly contrasts with the cooler temperatures of the surrounding rural land. But what's the science behind this temperature disparity? Let's delve deeper.

- **Causes:**

  - **Concrete and Asphalt**: Sprawling across the urban expanse, concrete structures and asphalt roads form the very skeleton of modern cities. But their thermal properties have unintended consequences. Concrete and asphalt have high heat capacities, meaning they can absorb and store a significant amount of heat. During the day, they soak up sunlight, becoming reservoirs of heat. But it doesn't end there. Unlike natural surfaces, these materials have slow thermal release properties. So, as night falls, instead of rapidly cooling down, they gradually release this stored heat, keeping urban areas considerably warmer. The very materials meant to symbolize modernity inadvertently convert cities into slow-cooking ovens.

- **Energy Usage**: The hustle and bustle of city life are powered by enormous amounts of energy. From the overhead lights that brighten the streets to the engines roaring in vehicles, every ounce of energy expended eventually converts to heat. Moreover, densely populated areas have a higher concentration of vehicles, factories, and households, all of which collectively contribute to the ambient heat. Think about the warmth emanating from a car's engine or the hot air released from building vents – all these seemingly minor heat sources aggregate, further intensifying the UHI effect.

- **Waste Heat**: The advent of technology has brought comfort, but it's a double-edged sword. Consider air conditioners, the ubiquitous solution to sweltering summer days. While they make indoor spaces cooler, the process isn't without side effects. Air conditioners work by absorbing heat from inside a building and expelling it outside. This expulsion contributes to the surrounding warmth. So, paradoxically, the more we rely on such cooling mechanisms to combat the UHI effect, the more we might be exacerbating it. It's a feedback loop: the hotter the outdoor temperature, the greater our reliance on air conditioners, leading to more waste heat, and consequently, even hotter outdoor temperatures.

In understanding the causes of the UHI effect, it's clear that human-centric urban designs, while aimed at fostering development and comfort, can inadvertently degrade environmental quality. Addressing this challenge calls for innovative solutions that integrate urban planning with ecological principles.

- **Combatting UHI with Urban Forests**

  - **Shade and Albedo**: At the core of the UHI problem is the extensive absorption of sunlight by concrete and asphalt. Enter urban forests. Trees, with their expansive canopies, cast shadows over these surfaces, effectively shielding them from direct sunlight. This shading reduces the intensity of heat absorbed. But trees play a dual role. Their leaves and branches have a higher albedo or reflectivity, as compared to concrete or asphalt. By reflecting a higher percentage of the sun's rays back into space, they help in mitigating the overall heat retained by urban surfaces. In essence, urban forests act as nature's sunblock, warding off excessive heat.

  - **Evapotranspiration**: Beyond just providing shade, trees have an intrinsic cooling mechanism. Through a process known as evapotranspiration, trees take up water from the soil and release it as water vapor from their leaves. As this water vapor rises and disperses, it absorbs and dissipates heat from the surrounding environment, providing a natural air-conditioning effect. It's not just about having a few isolated trees; a cluster of them can create microclimates, pockets of cooler air amidst the urban heat.

  - **Strategic Planting**: Harnessing the benefits of urban forests requires more than just sporadic tree planting. Strategic planting is crucial. By positioning trees in areas that receive direct sunlight, especially near windows and building facades, the indoor temperatures can be significantly lowered. This naturally cooler environment reduces the dependency on artificial cooling systems like air conditioners. As a result, there's a double advantage: not only is less energy consumed, but the amount of waste heat expelled into the environment is also reduced. This symbiotic relationship between urban structures and trees exemplifies how traditional urban design can seamlessly integrate with nature for a sustainable future.

In an era marked by climate change and global warming, the role of urban forests transcends aesthetics. They represent a confluence of tradition and innovation, proving that even in the heart of concrete jungles, nature can flourish and, in doing so, shield urban dwellers from the escalating temperatures.

Sprawling Cities

Urbanization, in many ways, represents the advancement of human civilization. As technological innovation and economic opportunities concentrate in urban areas, millions are drawn to cities, turning them into buzzing hubs of activity. However, this rapid urban expansion, especially in the 21st century, comes with an ecological price tag. Cities, like hungry giants, constantly demand more: more space, more resources, more connectivity. This relentless demand has profound implications for forests both at the local and global levels.

- **Direct Encroachment**: At the forefront of this urban expansion is the direct consumption of green spaces. In the rush to accommodate a burgeoning population, especially in fast-growing cities of developing nations, urban planning often takes a backseat. Forested areas, wetlands, and agricultural lands at the city's edges become prime targets. As concrete structures replace these green spaces, the ecological ramifications are manifold. Native flora and fauna lose their habitats, leading to reduced biodiversity. Additionally, human-wildlife conflicts surge as animals, disoriented and displaced, venture into human settlements. An elephant wandering into a city or leopards being spotted in urban areas are not mere anomalies; they're distress signals of nature being pushed to its brink.

- **Resource Needs and Indirect Deforestation**:

  - **Water Consumption**: The thirst of an expanding city is unquenchable. To meet the escalating water demands, authorities often look towards rivers and streams, nestled in forested catchments, as sources. The solution frequently adopted is the construction of dams. While dams promise a steady water supply, they inundate vast areas, submerging not just forests but also the intricate ecosystems they support. Aquatic life, especially freshwater species, face the risk of extinction, and terrestrial animals are displaced, further exacerbating the human-wildlife conflict.

  - **Food and Commodities**: A city's appetite extends beyond just water. The daily influx of thousands necessitates a steady supply of food. To cater to this demand, forests are often razed to make way for agricultural lands, cattle pastures, or poultry farms. This not only decimates local ecosystems but also introduces pollutants, such as fertilizers and pesticides, into the environment. Furthermore, the urban demand for commodities plays a role in remote deforestation. The timber used in constructing urban high-rises, or the teak that becomes a part of luxurious furniture, often has its roots in forests thousands of miles away. The urban consumer, far removed from these extraction sites, remains largely oblivious to this ecological cost.

- **Infrastructure**: Connectivity is the lifeblood of modern cities. The labyrinth of roads, highways, bridges, railways, and airports that crisscross urban landscapes facilitates movement and trade. However, the creation of this infrastructure often requires carving out paths through forests. Such fragmentation disrupts wildlife corridors, isolates animal populations, and exposes the inner forest areas to external threats like illegal logging or poaching. It's a domino effect; the initial infrastructure development paves the way for further encroachments, perpetuating a cycle of destruction.

In essence, while cities symbolize human progress, their unchecked expansion poses one of the most significant challenges to global forest conservation. Balancing urban growth with ecological sustainability will be one of the defining challenges of this century.

Urbanization, while a marker of societal progress, comes with significant ecological costs. Balancing urban needs with conservation imperatives requires foresight, sustainable planning, and an acknowledgment of the intrinsic value of forests in our urban lives.

Role of Technology

Satellite Monitoring

The technological evolution of the last few decades has revolutionized our ability to observe and protect the planet's vital resources. One of the most potent tools in this endeavor is satellite monitoring. These sophisticated machines, orbiting our planet, provide a detailed, bird's-eye view of the state of our forests, turning the spotlight on areas undergoing rapid changes and offering insights that ground-level observations might miss.

- **Advancements in Remote Sensing**: The field of remote sensing has seen dramatic advancements in recent years. Early satellites could only provide coarse, low-resolution images that gave a broad overview of large-scale changes. Today, the picture is drastically different. Modern satellite systems, whether from government initiatives like the Landsat program or innovative private ventures like Planet Labs, can capture images so detailed that individual trees can be distinguished. These advancements mean that we can now detect even small-scale logging activities, giving conservationists a sharper tool in their arsenal.

- **Detecting Deforestation in Real-time**: Real-time monitoring was once a pipe dream for environmentalists, but no longer. Platforms such as Global Forest Watch harness the power of modern satellite imagery to deliver near-instantaneous alerts about changes in forest cover. The immediacy of this information is crucial. In the past, by the time deforestation activities were detected, the damage was often already done. Now, with real-time alerts, interventions can be swift, with a better chance of halting or even reversing the damage. Whether it's local communities, who can now guard their ancestral lands more effectively, or international organizations that can put pressure on offending entities, the advantage is undeniable.

- **Data Analysis and AI**: Of course, the sheer volume of data generated by these satellites is staggering. Every day, terabytes of images are beamed back to Earth. Analyzing this manually would be an impossible task. Enter artificial intelligence (AI) and machine learning. These technologies, which have seen their own exponential growth, are now being used to sift through the satellite data, identifying patterns, and flagging potential deforestation activities. The synergy of satellite technology with AI promises a future where illegal logging can be detected almost as soon as it begins.

- **Policy and Accountability**: The transparency offered by satellite monitoring is also reshaping policy and corporate accountability. Governments can no longer turn a blind eye to illegal activities within their borders, as satellite data provides undeniable evidence. Similarly, corporations, in an age of increasing environmental consciousness, can be held accountable for their supply chain practices. If a company claims to source its materials sustainably, satellite data can verify those claims. This is pushing companies to be more transparent and is driving the adoption of sustainable practices at an unprecedented scale.

In the battle to conserve our planet's lungs, satellite monitoring is proving to be one of the most potent weapons. As the technology continues to improve, its role in safeguarding our forests will only become more critical.

Blockchain and Traceability

Blockchain technology, which first gained attention as the underpinning for digital currencies like Bitcoin, has since expanded its horizons. Its unique architecture offers a level of transparency and security that many sectors, including environmental conservation, are finding invaluable. Specifically, in the fight against deforestation, blockchain offers a robust tool for ensuring that the products we consume have been sourced sustainably.

- **Transparent Supply Chains**: One of blockchain's primary benefits is its potential to make supply chains transparent. Given that it operates on a decentralized ledger where each transaction is recorded and confirmed across multiple nodes, it becomes almost impossible for any single entity to manipulate the data undetected. This can be game-changing for industries like timber or palm oil, where products often pass through multiple hands before reaching the consumer. By logging each step on the blockchain, from the moment a tree is cut or a fruit is harvested, through processing, transportation, and sale, there's an unbroken, verifiable record of its journey. This drastically reduces the chances of unsustainably sourced products entering the supply chain unnoticed.

- **Empowering Consumers**: Modern consumers aren't just passive buyers; they're stakeholders who, equipped with the right information, can drive significant change. With blockchain's traceability features, consumers can, with the scan of a QR code, trace the origins of their purchase. Knowing that a product has been sustainably sourced and that its journey has been logged on an immutable blockchain can influence purchasing decisions. Over time, as consumers favor ethically sourced products, businesses will feel the pressure to prioritize sustainability or risk obsolescence.

- **Challenges**: However, the adoption of blockchain isn't without its hurdles.

  - **Integration**: Convincing every player in the supply chain, especially in sectors with deep-rooted traditional practices, to embrace blockchain can be daunting. Small-scale farmers or loggers might not have the technical expertise or infrastructure to participate in a blockchain system. Bridging this gap requires education, resources, and sometimes incentives.

  - **Validity of Data**: A blockchain is only as truthful as the data entered into it. While it guarantees the security of data once it's logged, there's no inherent mechanism to ensure that data is accurate at the point of entry. This means that third-party verification systems, perhaps using IoT devices or on-ground inspections, are essential to maintain the system's integrity.

- **Certifications and Tokens**: To incentivize sustainability, some blockchain platforms reward sustainable practices with digital tokens or certifications. Companies can trade these tokens, use them for transactions, or showcase them as badges of honor, signifying their commitment to preserving the environment. Over time, these tokens or certifications can become markers of trust and quality, further driving the adoption of sustainable practices across industries.

In conclusion, while blockchain offers a powerful tool in the battle against deforestation, its efficacy hinges on widespread adoption and rigorous validation mechanisms. As the technology matures and becomes more accessible, it could reshape how industries approach sustainability and traceability.

Embracing technology is essential in the fight against deforestation. However, technology alone isn't a panacea. It must be coupled with strong policies, international cooperation, and a global commitment to sustainability. Only then can the tools of technology be fully harnessed to protect our planet's irreplaceable forests.

Voices of Dissent and Action

Environmental Activists

In the annals of environmental conservation, there have been luminaries whose dedication and perseverance have left indelible marks. These environmental activists, often emerging from the very communities affected by deforestation, have become symbols of resistance against environmental degradation, teaching the world about the value of nature and the need to protect it.

- **Chico Mendes**: Francisco "Chico" Alves Mendes Filho emerged from the heart of the Amazon, the world's largest rainforest, as a beacon of hope for environmentalists. Born into a family of rubber tappers, Mendes understood the intricate balance between humans and forests. He saw firsthand the encroachment of cattle ranchers and loggers into the forest, the land that his community had sustainably harvested for generations.

  Mendes' activism wasn't just about trees; it was deeply intertwined with the livelihoods of the rubber tappers and the indigenous communities. He advocated for extractive reserves, areas where locals could continue their traditional ways of harvesting without destroying the forest. His philosophy emphasized that the protection of the Amazon was not only an ecological necessity but also a socioeconomic one.

  His dedication to the forest and its people made him many enemies, especially among powerful ranching and logging interests. Despite numerous threats, Mendes continued his advocacy, drawing international attention to the plight of the Amazon and its inhabitants. His tragic assassination in 1988 highlighted the dangers faced by environmental activists but also galvanized international support for the Amazon's protection. Mendes' spirit and vision inspired a new generation of activists, proving that individuals could indeed make a difference.

- **Wangari Maathai**: Dr. Wangari Maathai's journey from a small village in Kenya to the global stage as a Nobel laureate is a testament to her indomitable spirit and belief in the power of grassroots movements. Maathai saw the devastating effects of deforestation in Kenya: rivers drying up, food supplies dwindling, and women walking farther to fetch firewood.

In response, she started the Green Belt Movement in 1977, an initiative that encouraged women to plant trees, thereby combating deforestation and providing them with a source of income. This simple act of planting trees became a powerful tool for community development, women's empowerment, and environmental conservation.

But Maathai's efforts went beyond just planting trees. She became a fierce critic of corrupt practices and policies that led to environmental degradation in Kenya. Her activism led to several arrests, but she remained undeterred. She believed in the power of collective action and often emphasized the importance of civic and environmental education.

Maathai's vision and tenacity have left an indelible mark. Today, the Green Belt Movement has planted over 51 million trees in Kenya. But more than just trees, Maathai planted ideas - ideas of hope, resilience, and the power of grassroots activism. Her legacy serves as a beacon for environmentalists worldwide, reminding them of the intimate connection between people, their rights, and the environment.

In an era marked by rapid deforestation and environmental degradation, figures like Mendes and Maathai stand out, not just for their love for the environment, but for their understanding of the intricate balance between nature and humanity. Their lives and legacies continue to inspire countless individuals to take up the mantle and fight for a greener, just world.

Conservation Groups

In the face of accelerating deforestation and its global implications, non-governmental organizations (NGOs) serve as the vanguard of forest conservation efforts. These organizations, fueled by passion, expertise, and global support, work tirelessly to stem the tide of forest loss, often filling the void left by governmental and corporate interests.

- **Greenpeace**: Emerging in the 1970s, Greenpeace quickly became a household name in environmental activism. Their commitment to peaceful protest and direct action has seen them tackle some of the world's most powerful industries and governments. In the context of deforestation, Greenpeace's approach has been multifaceted. They've documented illegal logging, supported indigenous rights, and exposed corporate practices that drive forest loss.

One of Greenpeace's most notable campaigns targeted the soybean and cattle industries in the Amazon, revealing their roles in deforestation. By tracing the journey of these products from the Amazon to global markets, they highlighted the complicity of major brands and retailers. Such campaigns don't just create awareness; they force corporate accountability, pushing brands to adopt zero-deforestation policies.

Furthermore, Greenpeace's in-depth reports and investigations provide invaluable data and insights into deforestation patterns, offering tools for policymakers, researchers, and other activists.

- **World Wildlife Fund (WWF)**: Since its inception in 1961, WWF has evolved into one of the world's leading conservation organizations. Their approach to deforestation is holistic, recognizing that saving forests isn't just about marking boundaries and keeping loggers out.

WWF's work in tropical forests, like the Amazon, Congo Basin, and the Greater Mekong, has involved collaboration with governments to set up protected areas and wildlife corridors. These zones act as sanctuaries for endangered species and biodiversity hotspots, ensuring the survival of critical ecosystems.

However, WWF also understands the human dimension of forests. They actively engage local communities, ensuring that conservation efforts align with their needs and aspirations. This community-based approach to conservation recognizes that the people who've lived in and around these forests for generations are their best custodians.

- **Rainforest Alliance**: Founded in 1987, the Rainforest Alliance's mission has been to transform land-use practices, business practices, and consumer behavior. Their certification system is a game-changer. By certifying products that adhere to rigorous environmental and social standards, they've given consumers a choice to vote with their wallets for a more sustainable world.

  The "green frog" certification seal is a testament to sustainable farming. It assures consumers that the products they're buying—from coffee to cocoa to bananas—didn't come at the expense of forests. But it's not just about protecting trees; it's about ensuring that farmers receive fair wages, that child labor isn't employed, and that farming practices are sustainable in the long run.

  Moreover, by working closely with companies to integrate sustainable practices across supply chains, the Rainforest Alliance bridges the gap between conservation and commerce. Their work demonstrates that profitability and sustainability aren't mutually exclusive but can go hand-in-hand.

In summary, while deforestation may seem like an insurmountable challenge, the relentless efforts of NGOs like Greenpeace, WWF, and the Rainforest Alliance provide a beacon of hope. Through direct action, collaboration, advocacy, and innovation, these organizations are not only conserving the world's forests but are also reshaping our relationship with the natural world.

Indigenous Movements

Indigenous movements worldwide are a powerful testament to the resilience, determination, and depth of connection that native communities have with their lands. These communities, armed with centuries-old wisdom and an intrinsic understanding of ecosystems, stand as bulwarks against the unrelenting tide of industrialization and deforestation.

- **The Kayapó People**: Nestled in the heart of the Brazilian Amazon, the Kayapó people epitomize the fierce and unwavering defense of the indigenous territories. Their ancestral lands, rich in biodiversity, are a mosaic of life, culture, and natural beauty. However, these lands have not been immune to the encroaching hands of illegal loggers and miners, attracted by the promise of wealth extraction.

  The Kayapó, however, have proved to be formidable guardians. They meld traditional knowledge, passed down generations, with modern technology like GPS and satellite imaging to monitor and guard their territories. The images of Kayapó warriors, adorned in traditional attire, standing defiant against machinery and exploitation, have become iconic. They are not just fighting for their land but are the stewards of a legacy, a complex, biodiverse ecosystem that holds secrets and treasures invaluable to all of humanity.

- **Sarayaku**: The lush, green expanse of the Ecuadorian Amazon is home to the Sarayaku, a Kichwa community with a profound spiritual and existential connection to their ancestral lands. When oil companies cast their eyes on these pristine forests, the Sarayaku did not just see an encroachment on their land; they saw an assault on their way of life, their identity, and the living entity that is their forest.

"The Living Forest" campaign transcends environmental activism. It's a worldview, a cosmology that sees the forest as a holistic, living entity. Every tree, every insect, every drop of water is imbued with life and spirit, contributing to the forest's intricate, balanced, and harmonious existence. The Sarayaku's resistance is a clarion call for recognizing the intrinsic value of forests beyond their economic utility. It's a plea for a paradigm shift that respects, honors, and preserves the intricate, sacred web of life.

- **Standing Rock Sioux Tribe**: The plains of North Dakota, where the Standing Rock Sioux reside, are a far cry from the tropical rainforests of the Amazon. Yet, the echoes of their resistance resonate with the universal themes of indigenous rights and environmental protection. The Dakota Access Pipeline, a symbol of industrial encroachment, was poised to not just scar the land but to penetrate the spiritual, cultural, and environmental sanctity of the Sioux's ancestral home.

The resistance at Standing Rock became a global focal point. It drew together indigenous communities, environmental activists, and allies from around the world in a collective stand against the extractive industries. The images of peaceful protesters facing down militarized enforcement painted a stark picture of the broader battle indigenous communities worldwide are engaged in - a battle to protect the Earth, uphold their sovereign rights, and preserve their cultures and identities.

In a world racing towards unprecedented environmental crises, the voices and actions of the Kayapó, Sarayaku, and Standing Rock Sioux are not isolated instances of resistance. They embody a global awakening, a realization of the intrinsic value of natural ecosystems, and the indispensable role indigenous communities play in preserving the delicate balance of our planet. Every stand taken, every tree protected, and every right upheld weave into the larger narrative of a humanity striving to rekindle its lost connection with the Earth.

The fight against deforestation is characterized by a mosaic of voices, from lone activists and local communities to global organizations. Their stories of resilience, sacrifice, and hope serve as beacons, reminding us of the urgent need to protect our planet's green cover.

Grassroots Movements

Local Success Stories

In the face of rampant deforestation, local communities have often risen as the unsung heroes of conservation. Their efforts, rooted in lived experiences, intrinsic connection to their land, and a deep-seated sense of stewardship, offer not just hope but tangible models for sustainable coexistence with nature.

- **Community Forestry in Nepal**: Nepal, a country known for its majestic Himalayas and rich cultural heritage, has been at the forefront of a quiet yet profound revolution in forest conservation. The concept of community forestry has transformed the way forests are viewed, managed, and benefited from. By transferring the custodianship of forests to local communities, the very dynamics of forest management have undergone a radical shift.

  Empowered by rights and responsibilities, local communities have actively rejuvenated forest landscapes that were once on the brink of degradation. The canopy is denser, the air purer, and the symphony of life richer. These revived forests are not just habitats for diverse species but also reservoirs of resources for sustainable livelihoods.

  A particularly commendable outcome of this program has been the rise of women as formidable forest guardians. In a traditionally patriarchal society, community forestry has become a vessel of empowerment. Women, leading many forest user groups, are not just conserving forests but reshaping societal norms and values.

- **The Green Belt Movement in Kenya**: When Wangari Maathai envisioned the Green Belt Movement, it was not just about planting trees; it was about sowing the seeds of change. With each sapling that found its way into the Kenyan soil, communities were reclaiming their lands, reviving their traditions, and fortifying their futures.

  This grassroots initiative, though humble in its beginnings, sparked an environmental and socio-cultural renaissance. Beyond the tangible achievement of over 50 million trees planted, the movement breathed life into degraded lands, enriched biodiversity, and bolstered local economies. Women, once on the sidelines, emerged as the backbone of the initiative. Through tree planting, they were not just restoring ecosystems but asserting their roles as leaders, decision-makers, and agents of change.

- **Reforestation in the Yucatán Peninsula, Mexico**: The Yucatán Peninsula, with its rich Mayan heritage, has been a testament to resilience and innovation in the face of deforestation. Local Mayan communities, deeply attuned to the rhythms of their lands, have undertaken concerted reforestation efforts.

  Drawing from a wellspring of traditional agroforestry knowledge, these communities have combined ancestral wisdom with contemporary practices. The results have been nothing short of transformative. Landscapes once scarred by logging or agriculture are now mosaic tapestries of flora and fauna. These regenerated forests are more than just carbon sinks; they are sanctuaries of biodiversity, archives of indigenous knowledge, and pillars of sustainable livelihoods.

Through their practices, these Mayan communities showcase that the path to conservation is not a return to the past but a harmonious fusion of the old and new, a journey where tradition meets innovation.

Challenges at the Grassroots

Grassroots movements, despite their deep commitment and invaluable local knowledge, are often David in a world of Goliaths. Their challenges, multi-faceted and persistent, highlight the broader systemic issues that define the battle against deforestation. It is crucial to understand these challenges not just as barriers but as focal points that need urgent intervention.

- **Land Rights**: Land, for many indigenous and local communities, is not just a piece of earth; it is a repository of history, culture, and life. Yet, many of these communities find themselves entangled in the web of legalities and bureaucracy. While they might have lived, thrived, and protected a piece of land for countless generations, the absence of formal land rights often renders them "encroachers" on their ancestral lands.

  This lack of legal recognition becomes the Achilles heel for many grassroots movements. Powerful entities, be it multinational corporations eyeing a resource-rich forest or governments planning mega infrastructure projects, often exploit this legal loophole. The result? Forced evictions, cultural erosion, and irreplaceable ecological loss.

- **Financial Constraints**: The asymmetry in financial power is perhaps most visible when grassroots movements confront giant corporations or government-backed projects. While local communities might have unparalleled passion, commitment, and an unwavering connection to the land, their coffers are often no match for the deep pockets of logging, mining, or agribusiness companies.

  This financial disparity becomes glaringly evident in legal battles where local communities struggle to afford legal representation. It also hampers their ability to invest in technology, training, or resources that can amplify their conservation efforts.

- **External Pressures**: Globalization, with all its merits, has also brought in its wake immense pressures on local ecosystems. Commodities that fetch high prices on the global market can tempt even the most eco-conscious communities. The lure of palm oil profits, for instance, can sometimes overshadow the long-term environmental and cultural costs.

  Furthermore, trade agreements, international policies, or debts can force countries to exploit their natural resources, indirectly pressuring grassroots movements that stand in the way of rampant deforestation.

- **Reprisals and Threats**: The battle at the grassroots is not just against deforestation; it is often a battle for survival. Activists, community leaders, and even entire villages that dare to resist deforestation become targets. Their resistance is met with threats, intimidation, violence, and, in the direst of cases, assassination.

The shadows of activists like Chico Mendes or Berta Cáceres, who paid the ultimate price for their resistance, loom large. Their tragic fates underscore the high stakes involved in grassroots movements. For many, defending their forests isn't just an act of environmental conservation; it is an act of unparalleled bravery in the face of life-threatening dangers.

Grassroots movements underscore the principle that those closest to the forest often care for it the most. Their successes and challenges provide invaluable lessons. To achieve global conservation goals, it's imperative to listen to, support, and amplify these local voices, weaving their knowledge and passion into a global tapestry of forest protection.

Alternatives to Deforestation

Sustainable Forestry

The increasing global demand for timber, paper, and other forest products has made the forest industry one of the major players in deforestation. However, when approached with an ecological mindset, logging can coexist with conservation. Sustainable forestry is not just an alternative; it's a paradigm shift in how we view and manage our forest resources.

- **Selective Logging**: Traditional logging practices, which involve clear-cutting vast areas, leave behind barren landscapes, disrupted habitats, and broken ecosystems. But what if we adopted a more discerning approach? Selective logging is akin to surgical precision in the world of forestry. By identifying and removing only specific, mature trees, the overall integrity of the forest is maintained. Younger trees continue to grow, animal habitats aren't extensively disrupted, and the forest remains a functional ecosystem. It's a methodology that respects the intricate interdependencies within a forest. Over time, with proper management, selectively logged forests can recover and continue to serve both ecological and economic purposes.

- **Certification Programs**: In a world of abundant choices, how does one discern between a product that's linked to destructive logging and one that's responsibly sourced? This is where certification programs come into play. Organizations like the FSC and PEFC have stringent criteria for what constitutes "sustainable" forestry. Timber products that bear their certification marks give consumers the confidence that they're supporting responsible forestry practices. These certifications aren't just stamps on a product; they represent a commitment to a certain standard of forest management that emphasizes ecological balance, social responsibility, and long-term economic viability. For companies, getting certified can also mean better market access, premium prices, and a positive brand image.

- **Riparian Buffers**: Waterways within and around forests are lifelines for numerous species. They're vital for the migration of fish, serve as drinking sources for animals, and play a key role in maintaining the forest's overall health. But logging activities, if done indiscriminately, can wreak havoc on these water bodies. Soil erosion from cleared areas can silt up rivers and streams, affecting aquatic life. Chemicals used in logging can pollute these waters. Riparian buffers, which involve leaving a protective belt of vegetation around waterways, act as natural safeguards. They stabilize riverbanks, reduce the runoff of pollutants, and provide shaded areas that are crucial for certain aquatic species. Beyond the immediate ecological benefits, these buffers also offer scenic beauty and recreational opportunities for humans.

Agroforestry and Sustainable Agriculture

The juxtaposition of agriculture and forestry isn't as common as it should be. The prevailing model of large-scale monoculture farming, characterized by extensive fields of a single crop, often ignores the multifaceted benefits that a more integrated approach can provide. Agroforestry, which merges trees and crops, paints a different picture, where food production and forest conservation aren't mutually exclusive but can be synergistically combined.

- **Benefits**: When you step into an agroforestry system, it's akin to entering a living, breathing biotic system where everything, from the soil underfoot to the canopy overhead, is part of a delicately balanced dance of ecological harmony.

  - **Soil Health**: Trees are the guardians of the soil. Their roots hold it together, preventing erosion and loss of topsoil, especially during heavy rains. But that's just the beginning. The presence of trees enriches soil structure and enhances its nutrient content, thanks to the decomposition of fallen leaves and other organic matter. Farmers find that their crops grow healthier and more robust in the enriched soil, leading to increased agricultural yields in the long term and a reduction in the need for chemical fertilizers.

  - **Biodiversity**: In an agroforestry landscape, biodiversity blooms. Trees provide habitats for a myriad of species, from birds nesting in their branches to insects thriving in their bark. This coexistence of multiple species fosters an ecological balance, leading to a more resilient and adaptive ecosystem capable of withstanding pests and diseases naturally.

  - **Natural Pest Control**: Speaking of pests, the diversity of an agroforestry system is its own defense mechanism. With natural predators present, pest populations are kept in check, reducing the need for chemical pesticides. This not only lowers the costs for farmers but also mitigates the environmental impacts associated with pesticide use.

- **Carbon Sequestration**: In the age of climate change, every tree counts. Trees interspersed within agricultural landscapes aren't just providers of shade and habitats; they are silent warriors in the fight against global warming. They act as carbon sinks, absorbing and storing carbon dioxide, and thereby offsetting greenhouse gas emissions.

- **Examples**: Real-world applications of agroforestry offer glimpses into its potential for transforming agricultural practices and conserving forests.

  - **Shade-Grown Coffee**: Picture a coffee plantation where the coffee shrubs are nestled under a canopy of diverse tree species. It's not just an aesthetic choice but a conscious decision to embrace ecological coexistence. Shade-grown coffee is renowned for producing high-quality, aromatic coffee beans. But beyond the brew, there's an environmental narrative. The trees protect biodiversity, offering habitats to birds and insects, some of which are natural pest controllers. The soil is healthier, enriched by the organic matter from the trees. It's a holistic model where the coffee grows in harmony with the environment rather than at its expense.

The adoption of agroforestry and sustainable agriculture can be seen as a reclamation of age-old wisdom, a return to practices that respect the intricate interconnections within ecosystems. It's a rejection of the notion that productivity and conservation are at odds. With every tree planted amid crops, we're sowing the seeds for a future where forests and agriculture thrive side by side, where our food systems are resilient, diverse, and harmoniously integrated with the natural world.

Ecotourism

In the spectrum of conservation strategies, ecotourism occupies a unique space. It melds the allure of travel with a conscientious commitment to preserving the natural world. When done right, it not only offers tourists a transformative experience but also throws a lifeline to imperiled ecosystems. By turning forests into destinations of wonder rather than mere repositories of resources, ecotourism introduces an economic rationale for conservation, presenting a compelling alternative to destructive activities like logging or mining.

- **Community Engagement**: At the heart of ecotourism lies the principle of community engagement. When forests are viewed purely as resources, the indigenous and local communities that have called them home for generations are often sidelined or evicted. But ecotourism flips this paradigm. Instead of being seen as obstacles, local communities become central to the ecotourism experience. They offer guided tours, share ancestral stories, and impart traditional knowledge about the flora and fauna. This not only provides them with sustainable livelihoods but also empowers them to become frontline guardians of the forest. By ensuring that a significant portion of the income from ecotourism flows back to these communities, we can foster a sense of ownership and pride, ensuring that conservation becomes a collective, locally-driven effort.

- **Education and Awareness**: For many travelers, a journey into a forest is not just a break from their routine but a voyage of discovery. Ecotourism isn't merely about snapping photos or ticking off a checklist of wildlife sightings. It's about immersion, understanding, and connection. Guided tours, interpretive centers, and interactive sessions can provide tourists with deep insights into the delicate balance of forest ecosystems. As they walk beneath ancient canopies, spot rare wildlife, or hear the symphony of nature, tourists often undergo a transformation, becoming more aware of the significance of conservation. They return to their homes as not just travelers, but as ambassadors for conservation, spreading the word about the irreplaceable wonder of pristine forests.

- **Challenges**: Like all endeavors, ecotourism is not without its challenges. The very popularity of a destination can become its bane. Over-tourism can strain local ecosystems, with increased footfall disrupting wildlife, generating waste, and putting pressure on limited resources. Moreover, there's a delicate line between showcasing local culture and commodifying it. The commercialization of sacred rituals or sites can erode cultural integrity and dilute the authenticity of the experience. To ensure that ecotourism is truly beneficial, it must be pursued responsibly. This entails setting visitor limits, investing in infrastructure that minimizes ecological impact, and establishing a code of conduct that respects both nature and indigenous cultures.

In essence, ecotourism represents a confluence of conservation, economics, and cultural preservation. When orchestrated with care and respect, it can be a beacon of hope, illuminating a path where humans live in harmony with nature, celebrating its wonders, and cherishing its invaluable legacy.

Community-based Forest Management

The heart of any forest isn't just its towering trees, diverse wildlife, or the whispering winds that rustle through its leaves. It's the people who call it home, those who have shared an intimate bond with the woods for countless generations. Community-based forest management recognizes this intrinsic relationship and underscores the pivotal role communities play in sustaining forests. Instead of external entities dictating forest use or conservation strategies, community-based forest management champions the idea that the best custodians of a forest are often those who live within its embrace.

- **Local Expertise**: Every forest has its rhythms, quirks, and secrets. And few know these better than the local communities that dwell within or around them. Their understanding isn't just academic or theoretical; it's visceral, woven into their folklore, rituals, and daily life. Indigenous tribes might know which plants are best for medicine, when certain animals migrate, or how to predict weather changes based on the behavior of the forest. This deep-rooted knowledge is a treasure trove, honed over millennia, and offers insights that satellite imagery or scientific surveys might miss. By merging this traditional wisdom with contemporary conservation techniques, a holistic and effective forest management strategy can emerge. It's a synergy where ancient practices meet modern science, and the results can be transformative.

- **Stewardship and Ownership**: A sense of ownership instills responsibility. When forests are governed by distant bodies or organizations, local communities might feel alienated, viewing conservation measures as impositions rather than cooperative endeavors. But community-based management flips this dynamic. It gives communities a sense of stewardship, ensuring they have a say in the decisions affecting their ancestral lands. This isn't just about conservation for the sake of biodiversity or global benefits; it's personal. The forest isn't just a swath of land; it's a provider, a cultural touchstone, a legacy, and an identity. When communities derive direct benefits from the forest, whether through sustainable harvests, ecotourism, or cultural events, their commitment to the forest's well-being is magnified. They don't just protect the forest because of rules or regulations; they do so because the forest is an inseparable part of their story, their past, present, and future.

In essence, community-based forest management is a testament to the power of collaboration. It's a paradigm where conservation isn't a top-down directive but a collective endeavor, fueled by local passion, expertise, and the unwavering commitment of communities that love, respect, and derive sustenance from the woods. In a world grappling with deforestation, such community-driven initiatives light the way, showcasing a path of coexistence, respect, and enduring care.

Economic Incentives

Money talks, as the old adage goes. In the intricate dance between conservation and economic development, the right financial mechanisms can dramatically influence the trajectory of forest protection. Just as economic pressures can accelerate deforestation—be it the lure of timber, agricultural expansion, or infrastructure projects—well-structured economic incentives can serve as powerful catalysts for conservation. Such mechanisms, when judiciously implemented, not only promote the preservation of forests but can also foster sustainable local economies, underpinning a win-win scenario for both nature and communities.

- **Payment for Ecosystem Services (PES)**: PES is a groundbreaking approach that recognizes the multifaceted value of ecosystems. It's an acknowledgment that forests are not just timber stockpiles but dynamic, living entities that provide a plethora of services, many of which have global implications. Imagine a vast Amazonian forest. Beyond its timber, it regulates regional rainfall patterns, acts as a carbon sink, hosts a dizzying array of biodiversity, and even influences global weather systems. Through PES, such invaluable services are assigned tangible economic value. Communities, or even entire nations, are compensated for the global benefits their local conservation actions provide. This ensures that those who bear the immediate opportunity costs of conservation—like not converting forests to farmland—are rewarded for the broader benefits they bestow upon the world.

- **Conservation Concessions**: Traditionally, concessions have been synonymous with extraction. Companies pay to tap into a forest's resources, whether logging its timber or mining its minerals. But conservation concessions flip this concept on its head. Instead of paying to deplete, entities pay to preserve.

Whether it's a government, NGO, or even a private corporation, they lease land specifically to protect it from destructive activities. It's an innovative approach, essentially turning conservation into a competitive, economically viable land use option. In regions where logging might promise immediate financial gains, conservation concessions offer an alternative revenue stream, ensuring forests remain standing.

- **Carbon Credits**: As the climate crisis deepens, the role of forests as carbon sinks becomes ever more crucial. The simple act of a tree growing sequesters carbon, helping counteract the greenhouse gas emissions that drive global warming. Carbon credits turn this ecological process into a financial instrument. Companies, in their quest to become carbon neutral or even carbon negative, can purchase these credits, effectively funding conservation or reforestation projects that offset their carbon footprint. This not only provides crucial funds for forest preservation but also integrates the value of forests into the global economic system. Moreover, it creates an avenue for corporations to demonstrate environmental responsibility, catering to increasingly eco-conscious consumers and stakeholders.

In conclusion, these economic incentives, when applied judiciously and transparently, have the potential to transform the landscape of forest conservation. By intertwining the imperatives of ecology with those of economy, they offer a pragmatic path forward in the quest to halt and reverse deforestation. Through them, the age-old clash between development and conservation can evolve into a harmonious partnership.

These alternatives underscore a fundamental point: valuing forests for more than just their timber. By integrating economic, ecological, and social dimensions, we can envision a future where forests and humanity coexist and flourish.

Government Initiatives

The role of governments in determining the fate of their nation's forests cannot be overstated. By virtue of their regulatory powers and their ability to shape policy, governments possess a unique capability to either halt the march of deforestation or unwittingly aid its progress. Historically, state-led initiatives have seen a mix of successes and failures, often influenced by the balance of economic development imperatives, international pressures, local politics, and genuine environmental concerns.

- **Legislation**: Comprehensive legal frameworks are foundational in determining how forests within a nation's boundaries are managed and protected. While virtually every country has some form of forest-related legislation, the effectiveness of these laws varies widely. For instance, Brazil's Forest Code, established in 1965 and later revised in 2012, is a double-edged sword. While it sets out legal parameters for land-use in the vast Amazon, the specifics of the code have often been points of contention. Critics argue that its provisions, particularly those allowing for land amnesty for illegal deforesters, could potentially encourage further deforestation. At the same time, the Forest Code signifies a government's attempt to balance agricultural interests with environmental concerns in one of the world's most critical ecosystems. The interplay between politics, economics, and conservation becomes evident in such legislative endeavors.

- **Protected Areas**: Establishing protected zones has long been a favored strategy for governments aiming to conserve natural habitats. These areas, ranging from national parks to wildlife sanctuaries, serve as refuges where ecosystems can thrive without immediate threats from logging, mining, or agriculture. However, the mere act of demarcation isn't enough. Effective management, robust patrolling, and consistent funding are essential to ensure these areas don't become "paper parks," protected in name only. The success of protected areas also hinges on engaging local communities. Without their buy-in and participation, such areas can become flashpoints of conflict, with locals viewing them as impediments to their livelihoods rather than essential conservation endeavors.

- **Reforestation Programs**: In response to the global clarion call for environmental restoration, many nations have embarked on ambitious tree-planting drives. India's commitment to restoring 26 million hectares of degraded land by 2030 and China's vast "Great Green Wall" project are prime examples. While such endeavors are laudable, they're not without challenges. Merely planting trees isn't synonymous with restoring ecosystems. The choice of species, the methodology of planting, and subsequent care are vital. Monoculture plantations, for instance, might increase green cover but fall short in restoring biodiversity or providing the same ecological services as natural forests.

In conclusion, while government initiatives play an indispensable role in shaping a nation's forest fate, the complexity of intertwined interests and challenges necessitates a multifaceted, inclusive approach. Collaborative efforts that incorporate indigenous knowledge, scientific expertise, economic considerations, and genuine political will are paramount for meaningful, lasting conservation outcomes.

International Agreements

With the relentless march of globalization, the fate of our planet's forests isn't just a regional concern but a global one. Deforestation in the Amazon can impact rainfall patterns in North America, and declining forests in Southeast Asia can amplify global warming effects far beyond their borders. Recognizing these interconnected stakes, various international bodies and a multitude of nations have come together to forge agreements, hoping to tackle the deforestation crisis collectively.

- **The REDD+ Mechanism**: The United Nations' REDD+ initiative represents one of the most ambitious attempts to turn the global tide against deforestation. While the basic premise of compensating nations for forest conservation seems straightforward, the execution is intricate. How do we accurately measure carbon sequestration across vast and varied forest landscapes? How do we ensure that the funds flow to the right channels and genuinely aid in conservation? How do we consider the rights of indigenous peoples who call these forests home? While REDD+ has faced its share of criticisms, especially from indigenous rights groups and certain environmental factions, its emphasis on conservation as a part of the broader climate change mitigation strategy has solidified forests as critical components in global climate discussions. Furthermore, REDD+ has paved the way for public and private financial investments directly into forest conservation, emphasizing the tangible economic value of standing forests.

- **Convention on Biological Diversity (CBD)**: While the name may suggest a purely ecological focus, the CBD's ambitions span the environmental, economic, and social spheres. Born at the Earth Summit in Rio de Janeiro in 1992, the CBD recognizes that biological resources fuel our economies and societies and, thus, need careful stewardship. The convention's goals underscore the intertwined nature of conservation, sustainable development, and equitable benefit-sharing. Every two years, the Parties to the CBD meet to assess progress, set priorities, and coordinate efforts. These gatherings, called Conferences of the Parties (COP), serve as crucial platforms for nations to share successes, learn from failures, and collectively chart the path ahead.

- **Trade Agreements**: In the complex tapestry of international commerce, where goods crisscross borders, the fate of forests often hangs in the balance. Palm oil from Indonesia, beef from Brazil, or timber from the Congo—all are products embedded in global trade networks. Recognizing the environmental impacts of unfettered trade, some modern trade agreements incorporate "green clauses." For instance, the European Union's trade deals often emphasize sustainability, aiming to ensure that economic pursuits don't exacerbate environmental degradation. These clauses can range from promoting sustainable resource management to enforcing anti-deforestation standards. While enforcing and monitoring these provisions present challenges, their inclusion marks a significant shift in recognizing the inextricable links between trade, environment, and sustainability.

In conclusion, while the international agreements underscore a collective will to combat deforestation, their efficacy often hinges on local implementation, political will, and the complex interplay of economic interests. Yet, in a world that's more interconnected than ever, these agreements serve as vital frameworks, reminding us that forests are a shared global heritage, deserving of unified protection and preservation.

Challenges in Implementation

Policies, international accords, and strategic plans provide the framework for addressing deforestation. However, the bridge between well-intentioned policy and tangible results on the ground is often riddled with pitfalls. Transforming policy into practice demands more than mere legislation; it requires the synergy of political will, community involvement, financial resources, and vigilance against vested interests. Several impediments stand in the way of these ideals.

- **Lobbying and Corporate Influence**: The intersection of politics and business is a long-standing feature of many political landscapes, especially in democracies. Industrial groups, representing sectors like logging, agribusiness, and mining, wield substantial financial power. Their lobbying efforts, often channeled through substantial campaign donations or promises of job creation, can significantly shape legislative outcomes.

The consequence is that environmental regulations may be framed, not from the standpoint of ecological sustainability, but through the lens of economic gains. Such influence not only dilutes potentially robust protective measures but can also lead to policies that actively encourage deforestation.

- **Corruption**: Where governance structures are weak, corruption can corrode the very foundations of conservation initiatives. This malfeasance isn't just restricted to petty bribery. It extends to grand corruption schemes, involving high-ranking officials facilitating illicit activities that desecrate forests. From clandestine logging permits to turning a blind eye to obvious environmental transgressions, corruption allows profiteers to bypass the rule of law and continue their destructive practices with impunity.

- **Enforcement**: Drafting a law is one thing; ensuring its implementation is another. Many nations, particularly those with expansive and remote forested regions, grapple with enforcement challenges. Insufficient personnel, limited logistical resources, and lack of training can cripple on-ground conservation efforts. Moreover, in regions where local communities view conservation regulations as antagonistic to their livelihoods, enforcing these laws becomes even more challenging.

- **Conflicting Policies**: Governments, like any large entities, can sometimes work at cross-purposes. For instance, while an environmental ministry might spearhead reforestation initiatives, the agriculture ministry might incentivize clearing forests for farmland. Such policy disconnects can confuse stakeholders and undermine the effectiveness of conservation measures.

- **Land Rights Ambiguity**: Land ownership and rights can be a convoluted web, especially in countries with a colonial past or those with strong indigenous presences. Often, the lack of clear titles or formal documentation leaves local and indigenous communities in vulnerable positions. They face the risk of eviction or may find their ancestral lands handed over for commercial activities. This not only threatens the very fabric of their existence but also endangers the forests they have protected for generations.

In conclusion, while the challenges are manifold, acknowledging them is the first step toward formulating effective strategies. Addressing each impediment requires tailored solutions, collaborative efforts, and unwavering commitment. Only then can the tide of deforestation be truly halted.

In the intricate dance of policy, politics, and power, forests stand at a critical juncture. It's evident that mere policy-making isn't enough. The political will, backed by an informed and active citizenry, and balanced power dynamics are crucial to turn policies into palpable, positive outcomes for our planet's forests.

Controversies and Debates

Biofuels

Biofuels, heralded as the "green" successors to traditional fossil fuels, are derived from biological matter such as plants. Their emergence on the global energy scene has stirred significant debate among policymakers, environmentalists, and industry stakeholders. The nuances of this debate shed light on the challenges of transitioning to sustainable energy solutions while safeguarding ecological and human needs.

- **Pros:**

  - **Reduced Greenhouse Gas Emissions**: The carbon cycle of biofuels is fundamentally different from fossil fuels. When plants grow, they absorb carbon dioxide from the atmosphere through photosynthesis. When these plants are then converted to biofuels and burned, they release this same carbon dioxide back into the atmosphere. Theoretically, this results in a net zero carbon emission, given the carbon absorbed and released is roughly equivalent. On the other hand, fossil fuels release carbon that has been sequestered underground for millions of years, increasing the net carbon dioxide in the atmosphere and accelerating climate change.

  - **Renewability**: The word 'finite' is synonymous with fossil fuels. Earth's oil, coal, and natural gas reserves are dwindling and are subject to eventual depletion. Biofuels, however, offer the promise of renewability. Plants used in biofuel production—like corn, sugarcane, or algae—can be harvested, replanted, and harvested again in continuous cycles. This sustainable loop contrasts sharply with the extract-and-deplete model of fossil fuels.

- **Cons:**

  - **Deforestation Driver**: Biofuel's dark shadow often falls on the world's forests. The lucrative allure of biofuel crop cultivation, notably palm oil in Southeast Asia and soy in South America, has led to alarming rates of forest clearance. Vast, biodiverse-rich rainforests are bulldozed to pave the way for expansive mono-cropped plantations. These actions are paradoxical. While biofuels are pursued for their 'green' credentials, their production is facilitating the destruction of carbon-sequestering forests, leading to massive carbon releases and biodiversity loss.

  - **Food vs. Fuel**: The biofuel debate has another dimension—human sustenance. The lands used for biofuel crop cultivation are often the same fertile grounds suitable for food crops. As more acreage is dedicated to biofuels, there's rising concern about the diversion of critical resources—land and water—away from food production. This competition can escalate food prices, making staples unaffordable for many, especially in developing nations. The moral conundrum becomes evident: is it justifiable to prioritize fuel over food, especially in a world where millions still grapple with food insecurity?

In sum, the biofuel discourse exemplifies the complexity of sustainable solutions in our modern world. While their potential to replace fossil fuels and reduce greenhouse gas emissions is undeniable, the unintended environmental and social ramifications call for a careful, holistic approach to their adoption.

Genetically Modified (GM) Trees

In the quest to address the myriad challenges posed by deforestation and to cater to the ever-increasing demands of global industries, biotechnology has paved the way for the introduction of genetically modified (GM) trees. These are trees whose DNA has been altered using genetic engineering techniques to introduce favorable traits. While the advantages of such innovations seem promising, they are also met with deep-seated reservations from various sectors. Let's delve deeper into the pros and cons of this controversial subject.

Pros:

- **Increased Productivity**: One of the primary motivations behind developing GM trees is the promise of increased yield. Through genetic modifications, trees can be engineered to achieve faster growth rates than their non-GM counterparts. Theoretically, faster-growing trees mean more timber yield in a shorter span, which could alleviate pressures on existing natural forests. With the world's voracious appetite for wood and paper products, having a source that matures rapidly could serve as a buffer, preventing or reducing the need to fell natural, old-growth forests.

- **Pest Resistance**: Pests and diseases can decimate vast tracts of forests within a short period. Traditional forestry often resorts to chemical pesticides, which come with their own environmental baggage. GM trees, however, can be designed to be inherently resistant to specific pests or diseases, eliminating or drastically reducing the need for chemical interventions. This not only ensures a consistent yield but also lessens the environmental impact associated with pesticide runoff.

- **Cons:**

  - **Biodiversity Threats**: Nature, in its millennia of evolution, has crafted intricate ecosystems where each species, no matter how insignificant it might seem, plays a role. Introducing GM trees into such balanced systems can be like throwing a wrench in finely tuned machinery. These trees, with their enhanced capabilities, might crossbreed with wild, native trees, potentially diluting or altering natural genetic pools. Such hybrid offspring could have unpredictable growth patterns, disease resistances, or vulnerabilities. Furthermore, with their engineered advantages, GM trees might become dominant, outcompeting and overshadowing native tree species, leading to reduced biodiversity.

  - **Economic Concerns**: The realm of genetic modification is not just a scientific one; it's deeply entrenched in patents and intellectual property rights. If the most productive or resilient GM tree strains are patented by large multinational corporations, it could give them undue power over the global timber market. This can lead to monopolistic practices where these corporations dictate timber prices and supply dynamics. Furthermore, small-scale foresters or those practicing community-based forestry might find themselves economically sidelined, unable to compete with the yields of GM trees or afford the licensing fees to grow them.

- **Ethical Concerns:**

  - **Playing God**: The debate surrounding the ethical dimensions of genetic modification is as complex as the science behind it. By venturing into the genetic makeup of trees and altering it, humanity essentially steps into a domain that has, for eons, been the exclusive preserve of nature. This raises profound philosophical and moral questions:

    - What gives humans the authority to make these alterations?

    - Is it hubris to believe that we can improve upon nature's designs, honed over millennia of evolution?

    - Furthermore, in reshaping the genetic destiny of trees, are we inadvertently claiming dominion over nature itself, going beyond our role as stewards?

These are not mere rhetorical questions but deeply existential ones, challenging our understanding of our place within the natural order.

  - **Unforeseen Consequences**: Trees are not isolated entities but part of a vast, intertwined web of life. Altering the genetic fabric of trees might have ripple effects throughout ecosystems. The concern here is not just about the direct, intended effects of the modification, but the myriad of indirect, unintended consequences:

- For instance, a GM tree might produce pollen that affects non-GM trees, leading to unexpected crossbreeding and hybrid species. What will be the ecological role and impact of such hybrids?

- Trees are host to numerous organisms, from fungi to insects. How will these organisms react to genetic changes in their hosts? Will they thrive, or will they be pushed towards extinction?

- The lengthy lifecycle of trees compounds these concerns. Unlike annual crops where consequences might be seen in a year or two, trees live for decades or even centuries. This means that any adverse effects might only become evident long after it's too late to mitigate them.

Moreover, the permanence of these changes is unsettling. Once a genetically modified organism is released into the wild, recalling it is impossible. This irrevocability demands extreme caution, foresight, and a deep respect for the intricate tapestry of life that forests represent.

In the final analysis, GM trees stand at the intersection of science, ethics, and environmental stewardship. As with many innovations, they hold the promise of solutions but also pose questions that challenge the very essence of our relationship with nature.

These controversies underscore the complexities inherent in our relationship with forests in the modern age. Solutions are rarely straightforward, and every choice comes with trade-offs. In navigating these debates, it's crucial to prioritize long-term ecological stability and the rights and needs of local and indigenous communities.

The Way Forward

Restoration and Reforestation

As the specter of deforestation looms large, restoring our planet's green cover has never been more critical. But true restoration is more intricate than simply sowing seeds. It's a holistic endeavor, aiming to rejuvenate entire ecosystems, restoring not just trees, but the myriad of life they support, the waterways they protect, and the soil they nourish.

- **Afforestation**: While the term might sound technical, afforestation simply means introducing trees to lands bereft of forests for prolonged periods. It's like introducing life to barren spaces. However, the process is not as straightforward as it sounds:

  - **Ecological Compatibility**: Not every tree is suitable for every region. It's paramount to select species that align with the specific ecology of the area, ensuring that they thrive and support local biodiversity.

  - **Socio-Economic Considerations**: The local communities must be involved and invested in afforestation projects. After all, they'll be the stewards of these new forests. Their traditional knowledge, combined with scientific expertise, can guide the selection of tree species and forest management practices.

  - **Long-Term Sustainability**: Afforestation isn't a one-off project. These new forests need nurturing, protection from pests, fires, and illegal logging, and, sometimes, thinning to ensure healthy growth.

- **Natural Regeneration**: Nature, if given a chance, often heals itself. Left alone, many deforested areas can slowly bounce back:

  - **Biodiversity Boost**: Natural regeneration allows for a plethora of species to return, creating a diverse and balanced ecosystem. Such diversity often makes these regenerated forests more resilient to pests and diseases.

  - **Soil Health**: As the forest regrows naturally, the soil undergoes a healing process. Organic matter accumulates, beneficial microbes return, and over time, the once-degraded land becomes fertile again.

  - **Cost-Effective**: Allowing forests to regenerate naturally is often more cost-effective than active replanting, especially in regions where human intervention is logistically challenging.

- **The Bonn Challenge**: The global commitment under the Bonn Challenge showcases an unparalleled ambition in our fight against deforestation. But why is it significant?

  - **Scale**: The sheer magnitude of the commitment—350 million hectares—is larger than the size of India. This isn't just about more green spaces but about reviving watersheds, improving air quality, and enhancing biodiversity on a colossal scale.

  - **Collaboration**: The Challenge isn't the undertaking of a single nation but a collective pledge of countries across continents.

This shared responsibility underscores the universal importance of forests.

- **Beyond Trees**: While the heart of the challenge is reforestation, its spirit lies in the ancillary goals: creating jobs, bolstering community rights, enhancing agricultural yields, and combating climate change.

In essence, the path forward, layered with challenges, is also lined with hope. Through global cooperation, informed strategies, and unwavering commitment, we can aim to gift future generations a greener, healthier planet.

Innovative Solutions

As the modern world grapples with the devastating effects of deforestation, it has never been more imperative to seek novel approaches that merge the power of technology with ecological wisdom. Today's innovative solutions are not only about addressing the damage done but ensuring that restoration efforts are faster, smarter, and more sustainable.

- **Drones for Reforestation:**

A flight of innovation takes to the skies with drones that hold immense potential for reforesting our planet:

- **Efficiency and Scale**: Traditional reforestation methods are labor-intensive. Drones, on the other hand, can cover vast areas in a fraction of the time, making the dream of reforesting large tracts more attainable.

- **Precision Planting**: Equipped with advanced sensors, drones can assess soil quality, moisture levels, and other vital parameters to determine the best spots for seed planting. This ensures higher germination rates and better survival chances for saplings.

- **Data Collection**: Beyond just planting, drones can monitor the growth of the forest, identify areas that might need attention, and provide invaluable data for researchers and conservationists. This feedback loop can continuously refine reforestation techniques.

- **Artificial Intelligence (AI):**

The power of AI lies in its ability to synthesize information, recognize patterns, and forecast trends. When applied to forestry:

- **Predictive Analysis**: AI can sift through a plethora of factors — from changing land use patterns to economic activities in a region — to predict deforestation threats with remarkable accuracy.

- **Real-time Monitoring**: With AI's ability to process satellite images in real-time, illegal logging activities or sudden changes in forest cover can trigger instant alerts, enabling swift on-ground responses.

- **Informed Policy Decisions**: Policymakers, equipped with AI-generated insights, can make better-informed decisions, ensuring resources are directed where they're needed most.

- **Miyawaki Method:**

Dr. Akira Miyawaki's unique approach to forest regeneration is a testament to the blend of traditional wisdom and scientific understanding:

- **Biodiverse Mini-Forests**: Unlike monoculture plantations, the Miyawaki method promotes biodiversity by planting multiple species in close proximity. This not only ensures a resilient ecosystem but also creates habitats for various fauna.

- **Urban Green Lungs**: Given the rapid growth rate of these forests, they're ideal for urban areas. These dense mini-forests can act as green lungs, offering city-dwellers a touch of nature and aiding in air purification.

- **Community Engagement**: The simplicity of the Miyawaki method allows for community participation. Schools, neighborhoods, and local organizations can come together to create forests, fostering a sense of collective ownership and environmental stewardship.

As we hurtle into the future, these innovative solutions underscore a pivotal message: with creativity, technology, and determination, humankind can mend the fractured bond with nature and tread a path of sustainable coexistence.

Consumer Power

In today's interconnected world, every purchase made reverberates across continents, influencing production processes, labor practices, and environmental conservation. The power of the consumer is an often underemphasized, yet monumental force that, when harnessed consciously, can steer industries towards more sustainable practices.

- **Ethical Consumption:**

The rise of ethical consumerism is not just a fleeting trend but a profound shift in how people relate to the products they buy:

  - **Beyond Labels**: While certifications like Rainforest Alliance and FSC are vital indicators of sustainable practices, they're just the tip of the iceberg. Ethical consumption also involves understanding the story behind a product – where it comes from, who made it, and the environmental and social costs associated with its production.

  - **Supply Chain Transparency**: More consumers are now demanding full transparency in supply chains. This goes beyond just the final product and delves deep into every step – from the sourcing of raw materials to production processes, ensuring that companies uphold ethical standards throughout.

  - **Supporting Local**: Ethical consumerism also emphasizes the importance of supporting local artisans and farmers. Locally sourced products often have a smaller carbon footprint, and buying them ensures that money goes directly into the hands of producers.

- **Awareness and Advocacy:**

In the age of information, consumers are no longer passive recipients but active participants influencing brand behavior:

- **Digital Amplification**: Social media platforms have empowered consumers to voice their concerns, share information, and mobilize collective action. Campaigns that gain traction online can put considerable pressure on companies to modify their practices.

- **Holding Brands Accountable**: Brands are now under the microscope, with consumers expecting them not just to commit to sustainability but to act on those commitments. Annual sustainability reports, third-party audits, and stakeholder meetings are becoming common, ensuring that companies remain answerable to their consumer base.

- **Consumer Forums and Platforms**: There are now numerous platforms where consumers can share reviews, not just about product quality but also about the ethical practices of brands. These platforms foster a community of conscious consumers, amplifying their collective voice.

- **Dietary Choices:**

The food on our plates is intrinsically linked to the health of our planet:

- **Understanding the Impact**: Beef production, for instance, requires vast amounts of land, water, and feed. In regions like the Amazon, this has led to extensive deforestation. When consumers grasp the environmental footprint of their food choices, it can lead to more informed decisions.

- **Beyond Meat**: While adopting a plant-based diet is a choice some make for environmental reasons, others opt to reduce their meat intake or source it from organic, grass-fed, and sustainable sources. Such practices can reduce the demand on intensive, forest-clearing cattle ranches.

- **Local and Seasonal Foods**: Choosing local and seasonal foods reduces the environmental costs associated with transportation and storage. Moreover, local foods often come from smaller farms that use more sustainable agricultural practices compared to industrial-scale farming.

The transformative power of consumers rests in their everyday choices. By voting with their wallets, attending to the origin stories of their purchases, and holding corporations accountable, consumers wield the power to pave a more sustainable future, making the act of buying a profound statement of intent and vision for the world they wish to inhabit.

The journey ahead is undoubtedly challenging. But, with a combination of technology, policy, grassroots efforts, and informed consumer choices, there's hope. The path forward requires global solidarity, innovative thinking, and a steadfast commitment to preserving our planet's irreplaceable green cover.

Epilogue: A Personal Reflection

Walking through a forest is akin to strolling through the annals of Earth's history. As a child, I remember visiting a dense woodland near my home. With every step, the city's distant hum faded, replaced by a symphony of whispering leaves and chirping birds. Massive trees, some older than the oldest human civilization, stood guard, their towering trunks and sprawling canopies painting dapples of sunlight on the forest floor.

One particular day stands out. Venturing deeper into the woods, I stumbled upon a clear, serene pond. At its edge, a deer sipped cautiously, its alert eyes scanning the surroundings even as it drank. The serendipity of the moment, the fragile intersection of human and nature, left an indelible mark on me.

But as years rolled on, change was afoot. The once distant hum of the city grew louder and more intrusive. Bulldozers and machinery began to encroach upon this sanctuary. The trees, once tall and proud, were felled, their timeworn wisdom reduced to timber. The pond where I had once witnessed the deer became a construction site, its serene waters replaced by the starkness of concrete.

The devastation wasn't just physical. It was emotional, spiritual even. The loss of this forest wasn't just about the disappearance of trees or animals. It was about the erasure of memories, experiences, and the deep-rooted connection many of us feel with nature. It was a stark, personal reminder of the broader, more insidious pattern of deforestation that plagues our world.

Through this book, my aim has been not only to inform but also to evoke. Deforestation isn't an abstract, distant issue. It's personal. It's the loss of childhood sanctuaries, the silencing of nature's melodies, the fading of memories etched in bark and leaf. It's the indigenous communities uprooted from their ancestral homes, the species pushed to extinction, and the ecosystems thrown into disarray.

But it's also about hope. Just as forests regenerate, so can our resolve. Through collective action, informed choices, and a genuine love for our planet, we can stem the tide of deforestation. As I reflect upon the forest of my past, I also envision a future where such sanctuaries are preserved, revered, and treasured. For in saving our forests, we save not just the Earth but also the very essence of who we are.

Conclusion

Reflections: The Journey from the First Tree Felled to the Last One Standing:

Deforestation is a mirror reflecting humanity's evolution, desires, and the unintended consequences of our aspirations. The act of cutting down a tree, simple in its essence, has evolved in meaning over millennia. In our early history, felling a tree was a symbol of survival, providing essential materials for housing, warmth, and later, for clearing plots to sow the first seeds of agriculture. It represented mankind's growing mastery over nature, and for centuries, forests seemed infinite, their vastness overwhelming.

But as civilizations grew, so did their demands. The age of exploration brought with it an insatiable hunger for exotic woods, like mahogany and teak. The industrial era accelerated the pace, with forests viewed as mere resources waiting to be converted into wealth. Today, in the age of global commerce and unbridled consumption, the act of clearing forests is frequently driven by distant demands, abstract markets, and invisible shareholders.

Yet, there is an increasing recognition of the price we pay for such progress. Every tree lost is not just timber gained; it's a piece of a larger puzzle we're discarding. It means fewer habitats for countless species, reduced carbon sequestration, diminished indigenous territories, and the erosion of nature's intricate web of life. Should the last tree ever fall, it won't be in silence. It will echo the collective choices of humanity, sounding a clarion call for reflection on the balance between progress and preservation.

Metaphor: The Tapestry of Life:

Our world, this breathtaking canvas of life, is akin to a masterpiece crafted over billions of years. Imagine Earth's biodiversity as a tapestry, a vibrant mosaic, with every thread symbolizing an individual element of our global ecosystem. This tapestry captures not just the visual splendor of our planet but also its functional beauty – the way each element interacts, supports, and balances the other.

But with every forest we clear, it's as though we're pulling at the threads of this tapestry with reckless abandon. A snatched thread might seem inconsequential in isolation, but it compromises the integrity of the entire piece. Over time, with each thread lost, gaps emerge, patterns distort, and the tapestry's resilience diminishes. If we continue on our current trajectory, we risk reducing this vibrant masterpiece to a tattered remnant, devoid of its original grandeur.

However, within this metaphor also lies hope. Just as a damaged tapestry can be restored by skilled hands, our planet too can heal with collective effort. By acknowledging the importance of every thread, by understanding the interconnectedness of life, and by prioritizing restoration and preservation, we have the chance to mend, to rebuild, and to ensure that the Earth's tapestry remains as awe-inspiring for future generations as it has been for us.

Call to Action: Becoming Guardians of the Green:

Forests, often described as the lungs of our planet, are crucial lifelines in ways more profound than we sometimes realize. They are not just clusters of trees; they are intricate ecosystems, repositories of culture, and sentinels of history. As these green bastions come under threat, the clarion call for guardianship grows louder. We must not only hear this call but act upon it with urgency. The stewardship of forests is a collective responsibility, one that is intertwined with our survival and legacy.

1. **Educate and Advocate**: The ripple effect of knowledge is profound. By arming oneself with information, you not only make informed choices but also become a beacon for others. Hosting community discussions, participating in environmental workshops, or even leveraging social media to share information can make a tangible difference. By advocating for policies at local, national, and international levels, you become part of a movement that shifts the narrative from exploitation to preservation.

2. **Support Indigenous and Local Communities**: Historically, indigenous and local communities have thrived symbiotically with forests. Their understanding of forest rhythms, species, and natural cycles is unparalleled. By supporting their rights, you're not just preserving a forest but also the rich tapestry of culture, tradition, and ancient wisdom. This might mean buying products that directly benefit these communities, advocating for their land rights, or even partnering with them for conservation projects.

3. **Consume Consciously**: Every purchase we make sends a message. Choosing products that bear eco-friendly certifications or are sourced sustainably can drive market demand for responsible practices. Further, reducing meat consumption, particularly from large-scale agricultural setups notorious for clearing forests, can have a significant

impact. Remember, every meal and every purchase is a vote for the kind of world you wish to see.

4. **Plant Trees, But Also Protect Them**: While afforestation campaigns have gained momentum, they should not overshadow the significance of existing forests. Mature forests house diverse ecosystems and store vast amounts of carbon, making their conservation paramount. Participate in community watch groups, support policies that prevent illegal logging, and raise awareness about the irreplaceable value of old-growth forests.

5. **Speak with Your Wallet**: In a world driven by commerce, financial contributions can be instrumental. Donate to NGOs that work tirelessly on the ground to halt deforestation. Support businesses that have embraced green practices, proving that profitability and sustainability can coexist. Also, divest from companies or industries that persistently harm the environment. As consumers, investors, and donors, the financial choices we make can either embolden destructive activities or empower restorative efforts.

Forests are not just groups of trees; they're the heartbeats of our planet. It's time to shift from being mere takers to becoming caretakers. Let's come together to ensure that the story of our forests is not one of loss but one of revival, resilience, and reverence. The tapestry of life awaits our collective stewardship.

In conclusion, while the challenges forests face are daunting, they are not insurmountable. With collective action, informed choices, and unwavering commitment, we can transition from passive onlookers to active guardians of the green. The future of forests, and in turn, our own future, hinges on the choices we make today. Let's choose wisely, act decisively, and usher in a verdant, thriving future.